Including
Lower-achievers
in the
Literacy
Hour

Using stories and poems

Collette Drifte

HOPSCOTCH
EDUCATIONAL PUBLISHING

Contents

Published by
Hopscotch Educational Publishing Ltd,
29 Waterloo Place,
Leamington Spa CV32 5LA
Tel: 01926 744227

© 2001 Hopscotch Educational Publishing

Written by Collette Drifte
Series design by Blade Communications
Illustrated by Cathy Gilligan
Printed by Clintplan, Southam

ISBN 1-902239-63-6

About the series

Including Lower-achievers in the Literacy Hour is a series of books aimed at enabling all children, regardless of ability, to access the learning requirements set out in the *National Literacy Strategy Framework for Teaching*. There are six books in the series, one for each of the Primary Years 1–6 (Scottish Primary 2–7). They are designed to be used by teachers or other adults working with lower-achievers in the mainstream classroom.

The books offer a structured approach which provides detailed lesson plans to teach specific skills and goals as outlined in the *National Literacy Strategy Framework for Teaching*. The lesson plans cover work at text, sentence and word levels and target a learning objective from each term's work.

Since lower-achievers often learn at a slower rate than other children, and therefore would have some difficulty in covering the whole year's work within that time, the areas and skills which cause the most problems for these children have been addressed. For example, concepts such as sequencing or predicting are included.

A feature of the series is the provision of several resource and generic sheets for each lesson, which are aimed at considerably reducing teacher preparation time. Permission is granted by the author and publisher to photocopy these sheets for educational purposes within the school or organisation that has purchased this book. The sheets are designed to reinforce the teaching point and offer the child an opportunity to practise the skill being taught. The lesson plans also offer several activities to further consolidate the point. These are designed to be done either with an adult providing close support or with a degree of independence.

The generic sheets can be used with the lesson plans as explained or used by the teacher in a different way according to the needs of the children.

On page 5 is a list of assessment focuses which can be used as an individual assessment record for the children. This page is also photocopiable.

About this book

This book is for teachers of children in Year 3 (Scottish Primary 4). It aims to:

- enable lower-achievers to be introduced to and enjoy a wide range of stories and poems;
- focus on concepts that are essential for the wider development of the literacy skills of lower-achievers;
- encourage lower-achievers to tackle challenging and diverse tasks;
- enable lower-achievers to access aspects of the *National Literacy Strategy Framework for Teaching*.

The book should be seen, however, as part of a wider strategy by the teacher to address the difficulties of lower-achievers. Such children need a great deal of repetition, practice and consolidation. Therefore, the teacher needs to utilise as many resources as possible to ensure a varied approach which offers these.

The professional audience using this book covers a vast range, from the Newly Qualified Teacher facing their first class, to the 'old hands' who have many years' experience behind them and from the teacher who has never worked with lower-achievers before, to the Classroom Assistant who has worked with such children for a long time. Therefore, any scripting or suggestions regarding the delivery of a teaching point can be easily adapted (or even disregarded!) to suit the individual needs of the professional and/or children in question. The whole essence of teaching lower-achievers is to offer individualism and flexibility.

Chapter content

There are three suggested lesson plans in the 'story' chapters and two in the 'poetry' chapters.

Overall aims

These outline the aims for the lessons set out in each chapter.

Featured book/poems

For stories, this section names the book being used, the author and a brief synopsis of the story.

In the case of a poetry chapter, it lists the poems being used, the poet and the page number where there is a photocopiable version of the poems. This can be enlarged for shared reading in the whole-class session.

A feature of all the lesson plans is that the teaching points can be repeated using other texts or poems of the teacher's choice. This is useful if the chosen text is not favoured by the teacher, or if they need to provide more repetition and consolidation of a teaching point.

Intended learning

This sets out the specific aims for each individual lesson within the chapter.

With the whole class

This outlines a whole-class introduction to the lesson. Because the class is together at this point, the lower-achievers will have the support of their peers and also the opportunity to follow the answers to any questions raised by the other children.

With the lower-achievers

This is the main body of the lesson, since it is designed to be done with the lower-achieving group. The adult-led activities are designed to be done together with an adult closely supporting. The activities are designed to utilise an adult, not necessarily the teacher. The independent activities are designed for the lower-achievers to do without as much close support and supervision. However, the term 'independent' does not imply that the child should be left totally unaided or unsupervised. This is something to be decided at the discretion of the adult/teacher, who will know how much the child is capable of doing without support. A lower-achiever may need help at any point in a lesson and should always have access to an adult to provide that help and support.

The activities suggested may be adjusted to suit the needs of the children. They are intended to offer a variety of ways of tackling the same teaching point and are not necessarily a list to be worked through. To cover all the problems of the children would be impossible, so professional judgement has to be used. For example, occasionally cutting and sticking is required, which may be difficult for the child who has problems with motor control – here the adult can assist; some of the activities require writing, so judgement must be used whether the child needs a scribe.

Plenary session

This offers suggestions for what to do with the whole class at the end of the lesson in order to summarise and explore the learning undertaken in the lesson. This should not just be a 'show and tell' session but rather an opportunity for the children to demonstrate their learning. The lower-achievers should be encouraged to play a part in the session.

Acknowledgements

The following is a list of the books and poems that have been referred to or reproduced in this text:

Books

Henrietta and the Ghost Chase by Stan Cullimore, Young Corgi Books, 1994; *Granny Grimm's Gruesome Glasses* by Jenny Nimmo and David Wynn Millward, Collins/Jets, 1995; *The Owl Who Was Afraid of the Dark* by Jill Tomlinson, Mammoth Books, 1992; *The Thing-on-Two-Legs* by Diana Hendry and Sue Heap, Collins/Jets, 1995; *Omnibombulator* by Dick King-Smith, Young Corgi, 1996; *The Baked Bean Cure* by Philip Wooderson and Dee Shulman, Collins/Jumbo Jets, 1996; *Burping Bertha* by Michael Rosen, Andersen Press, 1993; *The Magic Finger* by Roald Dahl, Puffin Books, 1974.

Poems

'Mouse' and 'The Night-Time Monster' by Frances Mackay, published by kind permission of the author; 'Why is it?' by Max Fatchen from *A Third Poetry Book* compiled by John Foster, Oxford University Press, 1982, reprinted by permission of Max Fatchen/John Johnson (Authors' Agent) Limited; 'If your hands get wet' by Michael Rosen from *A Third Poetry Book* compiled by John Foster, Oxford University Press, 1982; 'Eskimo Lullaby' (Anon, Greenland) from *A Spider Bought a Bicycle and other poems for young children*, selected by Michael Rosen, Kingfisher Books, 1992; 'Sly Mongoose' (Anon, Caribbean) from *A Spider Bought a Bicycle and other poems for young children*, selected by Michael Rosen, Kingfisher Books, 1992; 'The Skyfoogle' (Traditional), adapted by Michael Rosen, from *A Spider Bought a Bicycle and other poems for young children* selected by Michael Rosen, Kingfisher Books, 1992; 'BED!' by Joni Akinrele, from *A Spider Bought a Bicycle and other poems for young children* selected by Michael Rosen, Kingfisher Books, 1992; 'Teef! Teef!' and 'I Don't Want to go into School' from *There's an Awful Lot of Weirdos in our Neighbourhood* © 1987 Colin McNaughton, reproduced by permission of the publisher Walker Books Ltd, London; 'Rockabye baby' by Max Fatchen from *A Third Poetry Book* compiled by John Foster, Oxford University Press, 1982, reprinted by permission of Max Fatchen/John Johnson (Authors' Agent) Limited; 'The Sound Collector' by Roger McGough, © 1990, from *Another Day on Your Foot* and *I Would Have Died*, Macmillan Children's Books 1996.

List of assessment focuses

Assessment focus	Chapter	Date achieved/comments
Can the child accurately sequence events, use question marks and exclamation marks correctly and tell the difference between 'there' and 'their'?	1	
Can the child use the term 'dialogue' correctly, recognise speech marks and discriminate syllables in speaking and reading?	2	
Can the child appreciate descriptive passages, correctly use the terms 'verb' and 'phoneme' and blend phonemes when reading?	3	
Can the child recognise and appreciate shape poems and use the term 'calligram' correctly?	4	
Can the child distinguish between rhyming and non-rhyming poetry?	5	
Can the child appreciate a range of story openings and use the terms 'adjective', 'singular' and 'plural' correctly?	6	
Can the child appreciate the endings of traditional stories, use the term 'collective noun' correctly and use the apostrophe for contraction?	7	
Can the child identify the main points of a story, recognise singular and plural personal pronouns and use the 'Look, Say, Cover, Write, Check' strategy correctly?	8	
Can the child appreciate poems from other cultures?	9	
Can the child use the terms 'capital letter', 'full stop', 'comma' and 'exclamation mark' correctly?	10	
Can the child recognise text written in the first person, distinguish between personal and possessive pronouns and identify short words within long ones?	11	
Can the child analyse the behaviour of the main character of a story, use speech marks appropriately in writing and use dictionaries and word banks efficiently?	12	
Can the child analyse the emotions of the main character of a story, recognise words that mark the passage of time and identify and use the long vowels correctly?	13	
Can the child appreciate humorous poetry?	14	
Can the child understand and use the term 'onomatopoeia' correctly?	15	

Stories for sequencing

Overall aims

- To use the text as a basis for exploring the sequencing of events.
- To revisit sentences with question marks and exclamation marks.
- To explore the difference between 'there' and 'their'.

Featured book

Henrietta and the Ghost Chase by Stan Cullimore (Young Corgi Books, 1994)

Story synopsis

There are four short stories in this book, featuring Henrietta, the mischievous hippo, and her family. Each story has a different plot – tricks in the library, a shared birthday cake, a spoilt computer game and cheating at chess. With the hippos' family life being remarkably similar to any human family with its squabbles and tricks, each story of how Henrietta's mischief never pays off provides amusement and entertainment. Each story can be used as a basis to repeat the teaching points without risking boredom or 'overkill' from using only one text.

Lesson One
. . . .

Intended learning

- To realise that the sequence of events is important for the sense of a story.
- To use the text and other texts as a basis for exploring the sequencing of events.

With the whole class

- Recite the lines of a nursery rhyme in the wrong order (for example, 'All the king's horses and all the king's men; Humpty Dumpty had a great fall; Humpty Dumpty sat on a wall'). Challenge the children to tell you why the rhyme does not make sense. Ask them to try to recite another nursery rhyme out of sequence. Write on the board the sequence they tell you.

Ask a volunteer to tell you the correct order of the rhyme and to come to the board and point to the sentences in the right order.

- Take a well-known fairytale and give the children a very short resume of the story, out of sequence. For example, 'Jack killed the giant and then he chopped down the beanstalk before throwing the seeds out of the window. Next he climbed up the beanstalk and then he took the cow to market.' Challenge the children to explain, in their own words, why this does not make sense.

- Explain how the correct sequence for any rhyme, poem or story is important for it to make sense. Discuss how each story has a beginning, a middle and an end.

- Read one of the chapters of *Henrietta and the Ghost Chase*. Ask the children to give the sequence of the story in a few sentences.

With the lower-achievers

With adult support

Choose from:

1   Explain again that stories must have a beginning, a middle and an end to make sense. Use equipment such as sequencing cards (available from LDA – Learning Development Aids) to practise correct ordering. Give the children a two-card sequence to begin with and then increase the number of cards per story.

2   Read the chosen chapter of *Henrietta and the Ghost Chase* again, letting the children follow the text and look at the illustrations. Encourage them to retell the sequence of events. Help them to write a sentence for each event on a separate sheet of paper. Ask them to illustrate and order these correctly.

3   Ask the children to tell you the order of things they do every day, such as getting dressed. Ask them to draw pictures showing the order in which this is done. Help them to write some words under the pictures.

4   Using Resource sheet 1a, ask the children to correctly sequence the pictures. Help them to read the sentences and order them. They should then match the sentences to the pictures.

5   Look at other simple texts together and discuss the order of events.

Teacher-independent activities

Choose from:

1   Give the children puppets with which to practise showing the sequence of a chosen story or rhyme. They should work in pairs or groups of three. Tell them they will have the opportunity to show their puppet story in the plenary session.

2   Ask the children to work in pairs to write a few words and/or draw a picture, for the beginning, the middle and the end of the Henrietta story.

3   Let the children complete Resource sheet 1a. Then ask them to cut out the pictures and stick them onto card in the correct order to tell the story.

4   Give each child a copy of Generic sheet 1 (page 113). They can either cut out the pictures and put them in order or write numbers by each picture to show the correct order. Challenge them to write some relevant words under the pictures.

Plenary session

■   Write on the board in the wrong order the four sentences about Jack and Jill from Resource sheet 1a. Read them with the children and ask them to tell you which order the sentences should be in. When this is agreed, read each sentence in order.

■   Talk about doing things in the right order, such as what they do to get ready to go to bed at night. What do they do first – get undressed, wash, read? What about making a boiled egg? Agree the order of how things should be done to achieve the perfect boiled egg.

■   Ask the children who used puppets to show the class what they practised. Then ask them to show their nursery rhyme out of order. Invite the children to tell you which is the correct version and why.

■   Ask if there is anything the children haven't understood.

Lesson Two

Intended learning

■   To revisit sentences with question marks and exclamation marks.

■   To use the featured book as a basis for exploring the use of question marks and exclamation marks.

■   To use other texts for exploring the use of question marks and exclamation marks.

With the whole class

■   Draw a question mark on the board. Ask the children to tell you what it is called. What are question marks used for? Where in a sentence will we see a question mark? Can they suggest some questions? For example, 'May we go out to play?', 'How old are you?' or 'Is it snowing today?' Write their questions on the board or let them write their own questions. Use a different colour for the question mark. Leave the questions on the board. Write 'question mark' on the board and read it with the children. Leave it up on the board.

■   Read a chapter of *Henrietta and the Ghost Chase*, showing the children the text. Afterwards, look through the story again together encouraging the children to point out the question marks.

■   Draw an exclamation mark on the board. Ask the children what it is. What are exclamation marks used for? Talk about instances when we might use exclamation marks. Agree some sentences and write them on the board, such as 'Mind that big hole!' Leave these up on the board. Write 'exclamation mark' on the board and read it with them. Leave it up on the board.

■   Ask the children to tell you other reasons for exclamation marks being used. For example, loudness, fear, warnings, amusement and surprise. Make a list and leave it on the board.

■   Read another chapter of *Henrietta and the Ghost Chase*, showing the children the text and emphasising the words or phrases preceding the exclamation marks.

With the lower-achievers

With adult support

Choose from:

1   Write two or three simple sentences and questions on the board without the question or exclamation marks and read them aloud with the children. Discuss together which ones need exclamation marks and which ones need question marks. Let the children come up and put in the punctuation themselves.

2   Read part of the chosen chapters of *Henrietta and the Ghost Chase*, letting the children see the text. Draw attention to the question marks and exclamation marks. Encourage them to look through the text with you to find some more examples.

3   Look at other simple texts together and encourage the children to read aloud, using the punctuation marks appropriately.

4   Using Resource sheet 1b, ask the children to identify the punctuation marks and then put the missing marks into the sentences.

Teacher-independent activities

Choose from:

1   Ask the children to look through other written texts (comics are a good resource for this) and find question marks and exclamation marks. Ask them to choose one of the pictures, copy or redraw it and write the text underneath it, using the punctuation.

2   Give the children copies of Generic sheet 2 (page 114). Ask them to write in the speech bubbles some questions with a question mark and some sentences that need an exclamation mark. They could use some that were written on the board during the whole-class session. Encourage them to think of some of their own. Alternatively, they could use Generic sheet 3 (page 115) to write these sentences.

3   Give the children copies of Resource sheet 1b to complete.

Plenary session

■   Ask someone to come up and draw a question mark on the board. Then ask for volunteers to ask you a question. Can they write their questions on the board?

■   Do the same for exclamation marks. Give the children a selection of sentences and ask whether they would have an exclamation mark or a question mark. For example, 'Get off my bike', 'Please may I have an icecream', 'Quick, run' and 'May I go out to play'.

■   Ask the children who completed a resource or generic sheet to show the class what they did.

Lesson Three

Intended learning

■   To explore the difference between 'there' and 'their'.

■   To become familiar with the use of the two words.

With the whole class

■   Write 'their' on the board. Do the children know what it says and what it means? Explain that this word refers to ownership by several people or things. Give examples such as 'They took off their coats,' and 'Their dinner was late.' Ask the children to think of some other examples. Write some of these on the board.

■   Now write 'there' on the board. Does anyone know what this says and means? Explain that this word does not refer to ownership of something but that it usually refers to a place. Give them some examples, such as 'I put it over there,', 'I went there on holiday,' and 'There is my bike.' Ask the children to think of some other examples. Write some of these on the board. (You might have to point out that sometimes they will find the word 'there' in a text when it doesn't mean a place. For example, 'Once upon a time there was ...' and 'There used to be a big tree here but it's gone now.')

- Teach the children a mnemonic to help them understand the difference. For example, 'I go HERE and I go THERE.' Both are spelled with 'here' and both refer to a place.

- Play a game where you say a sentence, such as *"Put your book down there"* or *"The girls want their sweets."* If the word in the sentence is 'their' the children should all stand up (or stay standing if they are up). If the word is 'there' they should all sit down (or stay sitting if they are down). See how fast they can react to the sentences.

With the lower-achievers

With adult support

Choose from:

1 Prepare a set of cards with either 'there' or 'their' written on each one. Then play a game of 'Choose'. Give each child one card for each word. Ask them to show you the correct card ('there'/'their') for some sentences. For example, *"David, which would you choose for 'The football team put on their boots'?"* and *"Manjit, which would you choose for 'The baby crawled over there'?"* Do this verbally first, then write the sentences on the board with the required word missing. Give reading help if necessary and then, together, write in the correct word.

2 Look at *Henrietta and the Ghost Chase* together. Ask the children to look for 'there' and 'their'. Help them to read the sentences they find.

3 Using Resource sheet 1c, ask the children to choose the appropriate word to complete the sentences. Give reading support where necessary.

Teacher-independent activities

Choose from:

1 Let the children complete Resource sheet 1c.

2 Prepare cards with 'there' and 'their' written on them and enlarge Resource sheet 1c. Ask the children to work in pairs. Child A reads out one of the sentences and child B holds up the correct card. If they are correct they write the word on the sheet. They could

then go on to make up some verbal sentences of their own.

3 Make a sentence game. Have prepared three sets of different coloured cards. On the first set write a verb, on the next set a noun and on the last set, 'there' and 'their'. Put them into three piles according to colour. The children take one card from each pile and have to make a sentence using all three words in which 'there' or 'their' is used correctly. If it is correct – and the others must agree – they can have a token. The sentences that the children think are correct should be left to one side to be checked at the plenary session. If a sentence is not correct, the cards go to the bottom of the piles. The winner is the child with the most tokens.

Plenary session

- Ask someone to come up and write one of the 'there'/'their' words on the board. Do they know which one it is? Challenge the children to give you a sentence with that word in it. Ask for other volunteers to give you some sentences.

- Write both words on the board and play a game where you say a 'there'/'their' sentence and someone has to come up and point to the word that is in your sentence.

- Check the sentences that the independent group made to see if they were correct.

- Make sure everyone understands the difference between the two words.

■ Put the pictures in the right order. Write the letters on the lines below.

A

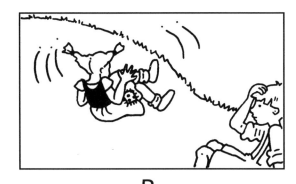

B

C

D

1 _____   2 _____   3 _____   4 _____

■ Put the séntences in the right order.

A Jill fell down the hill too.	1 _____
B Jack and Jill went up the hill.	2 _____
C Jack fell down the hill.	3 _____
D They went to get some water.	4 _____

■ Match the sentences to the pictures.

■ Match the labels to the punctuation marks.

exclamation mark

question mark

exclamation mark

question mark

■ What is this? 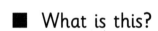 _____

■ What is this? _____

 Draw a question mark or exclamation mark at the
end of each sentence.

Dad shouted "Don't go near the water ____"

Sam asked, "May I go out now ____"

The girl called "HELP _____ I'm stuck ____"

"Would you like a bar of chocolate ____"

■ Write **their** or **there** in each sentence.

The boys put on _____ football boots.

The teacher said, "Put the books on the shelf over _____ ."

"We can go _____ tomorrow," said Mum.

The children opened _____ presents on Christmas Day.

Stories for dialogue

Overall aims

- To understand and use correctly the term 'dialogue'.
- To use the chosen text as a basis to explore dialogue.
- To understand how dialogue is presented in stories, through statements, questions and exclamations.
- To discuss the different ways that dialogue is presented – as speech bubbles or inside speech marks.
- To discriminate syllables in speaking and reading.

Featured book

Granny Grimm's Gruesome Glasses by Jenny Nimmo and David Wynn Millward (Collins/Jets, 1995)

Story synopsis

Everyone in Fiona Smiley's family is very brainy. She thinks if she wears glasses like them, she will be brainy too. One day, she finds a pair of glasses on her garden wall and puts them on. Unfortunately, she actually becomes Granny Grimm, the owner of the glasses, and undergoes some worrying and unfortunate escapades, until she can convince Granny Grimm's grandson to help her get back to her own home. This is made more difficult by the real Granny Grimm's reluctance to give up her new identity as Fiona! By the time she does get back though, Fiona has learned many new skills that her brainy family could never begin to tackle.

Lesson One

Intended learning

- To understand and correctly use the term 'dialogue'.
- To explore some examples of dialogue.
- To use the chosen text as a basis to explore dialogue.
- To revise speech bubbles.

With the whole class

- Write the word 'dialogue' on the board and read it with the children. Help them to say it one syllable at a time: 'di-a-logue'. Ask if any of them knows what it means. Explain that it means a conversation between two or more people. Ask for a volunteer to stand up and demonstrate a dialogue with you. Ask them a question such as *"How old are you?"* When they have answered, say that this was a dialogue between the two of you. Ask the children to turn to their neighbour and hold a short dialogue.

- Ask for quiet again and then ask the children to give you examples of where dialogue is to be found, for example on television, in books, plays, everyday life and so on. Explain that dialogue can be written or spoken.

- Read *Granny Grimm's Gruesome Glasses*, asking the children to listen particularly to the dialogue. Discuss a few examples at the end of the reading session.

- Point out that sometimes dialogue is shown in the form of speech bubbles. Do the children remember the work they did on speech bubbles in Year 2? Write on the board inside two speech bubbles 'How old are you?' and the child's response at the beginning of this session. Together read these aloud.

With the lower-achievers

With adult support

Choose from:

1 Give the children copies of Generic sheet 1 (page 113) and ask them to think about what the characters in the story might be saying. They could write the words inside speech bubbles.

2 Use 'Knock knock' or 'Doctor doctor' jokes to show how dialogue moves between the participants. For example, 'Doctor, doctor, I feel like a pair of curtains.' 'Well, pull yourself together.' Encourage the children to think of some others. Give each child a copy of Generic sheet 2 (page 114) and help them to write the jokes in the speech bubbles.

3 Using Resource sheet 2a, ask the children to read the speech bubbles in the pictures and then complete the dialogue by choosing the appropriate sentence from the bottom of the sheet. Give reading support if necessary.

4 Look through *Granny Grimm's Gruesome Glasses* together for examples of dialogue. Use Generic sheet 2 (page 114) and ask the children to write an example in the speech bubbles. Ensure that they are splitting the dialogue into its separate parts correctly.

Teacher-independent activities

Choose from:

1 Give the children copies of Generic sheet 1 (page 113). What might the characters be saying? They should write their speech inside speech bubbles on the pictures.

2 Ask the children to work in pairs and make up a short dialogue between themselves. Ask them to practise it for a performance. For example, they could make up a conversation about going away on holiday or playing a favourite game.

3 Let the children complete Resource sheet 2a.

4 Make a 'Knock knock' or 'Doctor doctor' joke book. Ask the children to work in pairs and write jokes to go into it, making sure that they separate each piece of dialogue correctly. You could give them Generic sheet 2 (page 114) for each joke.

Plenary session

■ Ask the children who made up and practised a dialogue to give a class performance. Write their dialogue on the board inside speech bubbles.

■ Ask someone to tell you what 'dialogue' means. Does everybody understand this?

■ Ask for volunteers to tell the class some of the 'Knock knock' or 'Doctor doctor' jokes. Hold the book up so that the children can see the dialogue in the speech bubbles.

Lesson Two

Intended learning

■ To use the chosen text as a basis to explore dialogue.

■ To understand how dialogue is presented in stories, through statements, questions and exclamations.

■ To discuss the different ways that dialogue is presented – as speech bubbles or inside speech marks.

With the whole class

■ Remind the children of the work they did on speech bubbles in the last lesson.

■ Look again at *Granny Grimm's Gruesome Glasses*, letting the children see the text. Show them how almost all the dialogue is presented in speech bubbles. Point to specific examples and ask, *"Who said this?" "What did they say?" "How did they say it?"*

■ Explain that dialogue can also be written in linear form. Write on the board two pieces of dialogue inside speech bubbles. You could repeat those you used in Lesson One. Now write them again but this time in linear form, inside speech marks. (Make sure you use a new line for each different speaker.)

■ Talk about the difference. Explain that it's very important to start a different speaker on a new line. (This is particularly important for the lower-achievers to understand.) Say that they will find both types of speech marks in different books or comics, but both show a dialogue.

■ Explain that dialogue can be written in different forms, for example as questions, statements and exclamations. Write these words on the board and on cards for permanent display. Remind them of the work they did on question marks and exclamation marks in Chapter 1, Lesson Two. Give them some examples from *Granny Grimm's Gruesome Glasses*, then give some of your own. Start with a question such as *"What time is it?"*, then make a statement such as *"I like this dinner,"* and finally make an exclamation such as *"I don't want to!"* How do they know which is a question and which is an exclamation?

■ Ask the children to think of some questions, statements and exclamations for you to write on the board. Make sure they are happy with the use of question and exclamation marks before going into group work.

With the lower-achievers

With adult support

Choose from:

1 Allocate roles in nursery rhymes such as 'Baa baa black sheep' or 'Mary, Mary'. Ask the children to recite these in role. Act as narrator when appropriate. (This may need to be done away from the main classroom.) Together, write the dialogues in linear form, using Generic sheet 3 (page 115). Make sure a new line is used for each different speaker.

2 Look at other texts, preferably familiar ones such as fairytales, and discuss the dialogues. Look for examples of questions, statements and exclamations. Discuss whether the dialogue is presented in linear form or speech bubbles.

3 Using Resource sheet 2b, ask the children to read the dialogues in the speech bubbles and then match the dialogue to the types given in the boxes. Give support where necessary. They could then rewrite the words in the speech bubbles in linear form using Generic sheet 3 (page 115).

Teacher-independent activities

Choose from:

1 Ask the children to draw a picture of Fiona Smiley as Granny Grimm talking to Sam Grimm. Ask them to write the dialogue using Generic sheet 3 (page 115) and the book as a model. Remind them to use a new line for each different speaker.

2 Have prepared three posters headed 'Questions', 'Statements' and 'Exclamations'. Give the children a selection of books and comics and ask them to find an example of each different type of dialogue and write these on the posters.

3 Let the children complete Resource sheet 2b.

Plenary session

■ Who can tell you what 'dialogue' means? How many different ways can it be written to show the reader that people are talking?

■ Ask the children what different sorts of dialogue they have learned about. Ask someone to give you an example of a question asked in the story. Ask other children for examples of statements and exclamations.

■ Ask the children who did role-play using nursery rhymes to show the class what they did. Act as narrator.

Lesson Three

Intended learning

■ To revise and understand the term 'syllable'.

■ To discriminate syllables in speaking and reading.

■ To use the featured text to explore syllables.

With the whole class

■ Write the word 'syllable' on the board. Ask the children to read what it says. Remind them of the work done in Year 2 on this. Ask a child to tell you what syllables are. When you are all agreed, practise clapping the names of some of the children to illustrate the point.

■ Now write someone's name on the board, breaking up the syllables with short dashes, such as 'Su-pin-der' or 'Tho-mas'. Ask one or two of the children to come up and write their own names in this way.

■ Say a familiar rhyme with the children. Ask them how many syllables there are in some of the words. Recite the rhyme, encouraging them to clap the syllables simultaneously. Write the words on the board and ask for volunteers to come up and write next to them how many syllables each word has.

■ Look at the opening page of *Granny Grimm's Gruesome Glasses*. Ask the children how many syllables there are in some of the words. Make a list of the words they suggest and the number of syllables each has.

With the lower-achievers

With adult support

Choose from:

1   Ask each child in the group how many syllables there are in their own name. Together, clap out the syllables for each name to check. Invite them to write their names, breaking up the syllables with short dashes. Help them to make a name chart with their names and syllable numbers.

2   Using Resource sheet 2c, ask the children to write how many syllables there are in each word of the nursery rhyme. Give help where necessary.

3   Make kites with 1, 2 or 3 written on them. Ask the children to write on the kite tails, words with the appropriate number of syllables for each kite. The children can look for their words either in *Granny Grimm's Gruesome Glasses* or in another favourite story. Hang the kites from the ceiling.

4   Make a board by drawing a large circle on a piece of paper and dividing it into four equal parts. Label each part, 1, 2, 3 and 4. Give each child a set of counters. Together, look at a chosen page of *Granny Grimm's Gruesome Glasses*.

Read it to the children and then pause at some of the words and ask how many syllables the words have. Each time, the children have to place a counter in the correct part of the circle to denote the number of syllables they think the word has. Use Generic sheet 4 (page 116) to write some of the words and the number of syllables.

Teacher-independent activities

Choose from:

1   Let the children complete Resource sheet 2c. Challenge them to find another nursery rhyme in a book and, by referring to the book, write the rhyme on the back of the sheet with the number of syllables in each word underneath.

2   Give each child Generic sheet 4 (page 116). Ask them to look around the classroom and write or draw some things they see in the appropriate columns on the sheet, according to the number of syllables. They can use the display labels in the room if independent writing is difficult.

3   Ask the children to work in pairs or groups of three to play 'Syllable Tiddlywinks'. Child A says a word and Child B has to give Child A the same number of tiddlywinks as syllables in that word. (They could use pictures to help them choose words.) Whoever has the most tiddlywinks at the end of the game is the winner.

Plenary session

■ Write 'syllable' on the board and ask for a volunteer to read it and/or tell you what it means.

■ Ask a child to come up and write on the board the name of a favourite person, such as a pop star or a sportsperson, writing the name broken up into syllables with dashes.

■ How many syllables are there in 'syllable'? Chant it all together.

Name _____

■ Look at the pictures and read what each person is saying.

■ Choose from these sentences to complete the dialogues.
Write them in the speech bubbles.

    I don't like meat.

    Come and sit with me, then.

    No, I want to play football.

    That's the same as mine!

■ Look at the pictures and read the words in the speech bubbles.
   Match the speech bubbles to the boxes.

statement

question

exclamation

■ Write the words in speech bubbles in sentences using
   speech marks.

_____

_____

_____

Name _____

■ Read the nursery rhyme and write under each word how many syllables it has. (The first line has been done for you.)

Humpty Dumpty sat on a wall,

   2   2   1   1   1   1

Humpty Dumpty had a great fall,

 __   __   __   __   __   __

All the king's horses

 __   __   __   __

and all the king's men

 __   __   __   __   __

Couldn't put Humpty together again.

   __   __   __   __   __

Stories for description

Overall aims

- To use texts to explore words and phrases that are descriptive and set the scene.
- To revise the term 'verb' and to use it appropriately.
- To revise the term 'phoneme' and to use it appropriately.
- To blend phonemes for reading.

Featured book

The Owl Who Was Afraid of the Dark by Jill Tomlinson (Mammoth Books, 1992)

Story synopsis

Plop is a baby barn owl, living at the top of a tall tree in a field. Unfortunately, he is afraid of the dark, in spite of his parents' best efforts to convince him that the dark is good. Eventually, Plop's mother pushes him out of the nest, telling him to ask other people he meets what they think of the dark. They all have a positive answer and, over time, Plop comes to have some good experiences of the dark. At the end of the story he is a fully-fledged, confident barn owl who not only is not afraid of the dark, but actually asks to go out in it hunting for food with his father.

Lesson One

Intended learning

- To use the text to explore words and phrases that are descriptive and set the scene.
- To explore other texts and find descriptive passages in them.
- To explore the idea of chapters and why they are used in stories.

With the whole class

- Write on the board some simple descriptive words, for example 'prickly', 'tiny' and 'skinny'. Read these with the children. Ask them to give

you some sentences using the words. What type of words are they? Explain that they are words used to describe something and to make the story more interesting and imaginative. Ask the children where they might find descriptive words, for example in stories, poems, magazines, newspapers and comics.

- Tell the children that they are going to read stories that are longer than many they have read before and that are divided into chapters. Explain what 'chapter' means.

- Read *The Owl Who Was Afraid of the Dark* to the children, showing them the chapter breaks. Encourage suggestions as to why books are divided into chapters. Do the children want to read on when a chapter has finished? Why? Explain about 'cliffhangers' and how usually a chapter ends at an exciting point, which makes the reader want to go on.

- As each chapter is explored, highlight the words and phrases that are descriptive. For example, at the beginning of 'Dark is Exciting', there is a description of Plop. Ask the children to tell you the words that describe him and write these on the board. Leave them on the board while working on this lesson.

- Ask the children to tell you other words they found descriptive and imaginative. Write these words on the board. For example, in 'Dark is Fun', there are words that describe the firework display. Ask them to tell you these words. Write them on the board.

With the lower-achievers

With adult support

Choose from:

1   Explore the words highlighted from each chapter again. With the children, make a word wall, writing a descriptive word in each brick. The children can fill in more bricks as they come across more descriptive words in the text. They can look at the words written on the board during the whole-class session.

2   Ask the children to think of their own descriptive words for other familiar situations. Encourage them to offer more than just one word. For example, instead of 'Sausages and

chips are my favourite dinner', suggest 'Sausages with crispy skin and chips that are crunchy and have lots of salt and vinegar are my favourite dinner'. Make a book together and help the children to write their descriptive sentences in it. Leave it somewhere accessible so that everybody can read it or add to it.

3   Using Resource sheet 3a, help the children to read the words that describe Plop. They should use these to write a sentence about him. Give support where necessary.

4   Give each child four descriptive words and a sheet of paper divided into four. (You could take these from the word wall.) They have to write one word in each section and then look in a simple dictionary for the definitions. They should write the definitions alongside the words. Give help where necessary.

5   While reading other texts, explore the descriptive words and phrases in them. Make a big book containing all the descriptive words that the children particularly liked. Let them illustrate the words. Leave the book where everybody can read it or add to it.

Teacher-independent activities

Choose from:

1   Ask the children to work in pairs. They should choose two or three of the words from those written on the board during the whole-class session. They should agree a sentence together, using those words, that describes Plop. Let them write the sentence and draw Plop.

2   Ask the children to complete Resource sheet 3a. If necessary, read the words with them first.

3   Prepare a set of cards, half of which have a simple descriptive word written on them (you could use the words on the board written during the whole-class session) and half of which have simple nouns on them. Place the cards face down on the table in their two piles. Ask the children to work in pairs to take a card from each pile and then make up a sentence using the two words. Explain that even silly or nonsense sentences are fine.

Plenary session

■   Ask for volunteers to come and write on the board some new descriptive words they discovered in their group work. Encourage the others to make up sentences using these words.

■   Let the children who made up silly sentences using cards with descriptive words and nouns share some of their sentences with the rest of the class. Which are their favourite descriptive words and why?

■   How many new words were added to the word wall? Read them together.

Lesson Two

Intended learning

■   To revise the term 'verb' and to use it appropriately.

■   To explore the text with specific reference to verbs.

■   To use other texts as a basis for work on verbs.

With the whole class

■   Ask some of the children to perform a simple action. For example, 'Martin, walk to the door,' or 'Yusef, sit on your chair.' Ask the rest of the children to tell you what the others did. Write their answers on the board – 'walk', 'sit' and so on.

■   Ask the children what type of words these are. If they suggest 'doing words' or 'being words', accept their answers as correct and then explain that the correct term is 'verb'.

■   Write 'verb' on the board and ask a volunteer to read it. Challenge the children to write examples of verbs on the board. Ask for some sentences to include the verbs and write them on the board.

■   Read a passage from *The Owl Who Was Afraid of the Dark*, asking the children to listen out for verbs. Ask them to choose three or four verbs from the passage and put them into sentences (verbally). Write these on the board.

With the lower-achievers

With adult support

Choose from:

1 Look through a chosen chapter of *The Owl Who Was Afraid of the Dark* again and together find the verbs. Make a giant poster of them. Ask the children to use bright colours to write them. Tell them they can add any new verbs they find to the poster.

2 Using Resource sheet 3b, ask the children to draw a circle around the words that are verbs. Give reading support if necessary. Help them to write sentences for three of these.

3 Brainstorm verbs on a theme, such as sport – jump, run, throw, kick, hit and so on. Make thematic posters containing the verbs. Use a dictionary to check the spellings and meanings.

4 Prepare a set of cards, half with simple verbs written on them and half with other words. Shuffle them and place them face down on the table. Each child takes a card and reads it. If they identify a verb correctly they may keep the card. If not, it goes back under the pile. The winner is the child with the greater number of cards at the end of the game.

5 Cut out the picture cards on Generic sheet 5 (page 117). Make some verb word cards to match these pictures. Play a game where the child has to turn over a picture card, say the verb and then find the word card that goes with it (or vice versa). They keep the cards if they are correct.

Teacher-independent activities

Choose from:

1 Ask the children to complete Resource sheet 3b. You may need to read out the words first.

2 Ask the children to choose two or three verbs from their current reading book and write a sentence for each one.

3 Prepare a set of cards with simple verbs written on them. The children should take it in turns to take a card from the pile, read it without the others seeing what it says and then do the action the verb suggests. The others have to guess what the verb is.

4 Cut out the picture cards on Generic sheet 5 (page 117). Make some verb word cards to match these pictures. Tell the children to play a game where they take turns to turn over a picture card, say the verb and then find the word card that goes with it (or vice versa). They keep the cards if they are correct.

Plenary session

■ Prepare part of the board to look like Resource sheet 3b. Ask for volunteers to come and draw a circle around the verbs.

■ Ask for volunteers to come to the board and write some verbs. Then ask them to suggest sentences for these verbs. Invite the class to remind you what verbs are.

■ Ask some children to come to the front and demonstrate some verbs. The others have to guess what the verb is.

Lesson Three

Intended learning

■ To revise the term 'phoneme' and to use it appropriately.

■ To use the text as a basis for revision and to practise use of the term.

■ To blend phonemes for reading.

With the whole class

■ Write 'phoneme' on the board and read it with the children. Do they remember what it means? Remind them of the work they did in Reception, Year 1 and Year 2. If necessary, explain that 'phoneme' means the sound a letter or group of letters makes. Ask the children to give you some examples of initial phonemes and then some final phonemes. Write their suggestions on the board and ask for some words that illustrate them.

■ Look at the title page of the featured book. Help the children to identify the phonemes that are in the title and the author's and illustrator's names. Ask them to blend some of these phonemes and tell you what they say. For example, ask what phonemes are made by 'Ji', 'To', 'li', 'in', 'on', and so on.

■ Look at some of the children's names and together work out the phonemes and blends contained in them. Write these on the board, both as a complete name and in the phoneme and blend components. Invite the children to read these aloud.

■ Play a game of 'Phoneme Football'. Divide the class into two teams and, using words on display around the room, ask individual children for the initial and final phonemes and blends. Correct answers score a 'goal' for their team.

With the lower-achievers

With adult support

Choose from:

1 If possible, use multiple copies of the featured book, or of any chosen text. Select specific words and ask each child to identify the initial and final phonemes and blends. (If you are sure the children have grasped the idea, ask them for medial phonemes and/or blends.) Let them write the phonemes and blends on the board. Together, find other words that begin with the same phoneme. Decide on a sentence for some of the words and help the children to write it. Ask them to use a different colour for the phoneme or blend being discussed.

2 Play a game of 'Phoneme Rounders'. Child A chooses a word and asks Child B for the initial and/or final phoneme or blend. If Child B is right, they take a token and then ask Child C, and so on. The winner has the greatest number of tokens at the end of the game.

3 Using Resource sheet 3c, ask the children to sound the initial blends. They should then match the initial blends with the given endings to make words and match these words to the pictures. Give support where necessary.

4 Give out copies of Generic sheet 5 (page 117). Ask the children to look in dictionaries to find how to spell the verbs demonstrated on the

sheet. They should write the words and circle the initial phoneme or blend for each in red and the final phoneme or blend in blue.

Teacher-independent activities

Choose from:

1 Let the children complete Resource sheet 3c.

2 Cut out the cards on Generic sheet 5 (page 117). Ask the children to take two or three of the cards (according to their reading and dictionary skills). They should then quietly work with a dictionary to find the relevant verbs, copy them out and circle the initial and final phonemes/blends.

3 Ask the children to work in pairs or groups of three to make a collection of small things from around the classroom for a table display. They should label the objects with the initial phoneme or blend.

Plenary session

■ Invite someone to tell you what 'phoneme' means. Ask some of the children to tell you the initial and final phonemes of their names. Ask for examples of medial phonemes.

■ Ask for some volunteers to come up and write two phonemes that blend. How many words can the class think of containing that blend? Write them on the board.

■ Ask the children who made collections to show the objects and the labels to the rest of the class. Encourage the other children to tell you what the phonemes and the blends say.

■ Read the words in the boxes. They say what Plop looked like.

fat

fluffy

round eyes

knackety knees

■ Write a sentence about Plop telling what he looked like.

_____

 Draw a picture of Plop.

■ Write another word to describe Plop.

_____

Name ______________________________

■ Draw a circle around all the verbs. (There are six of them.)

blue

jump

fly

run

Dad

dog

red

cry

play

yellow

cat

green

Mum

walk

■ Write a sentence for three of the verbs.

____

____

____

■ Read these blends.

fr   **an**   **sw**   **ig**   **pr**   **um**

■ Match the blends to the ends to make words.

fr	ts	ig	brella
an	eets	pr	loo
sw	og	um	am

■ Write the words under the pictures.

_____   _____   _____

_____   _____   _____

Calligrams and shape poems

Overall aims

- To explore shape poems.
- To become familiar with the term 'calligram'.
- To use the shape poems as a stimulus for writing own shape poems.

Lesson One

Chosen poems

'Mouse' by Frances Mackay, (page 30)
'Bananas' by Collette Drifte, (page 30)

Intended learning

- To explore shape poems.
- To become familiar with the term 'calligram'.

With the whole class

- Enlarge copies of 'Mouse' and 'Bananas'. Tell the children that they are going to talk about some poems in which the shape of the poem plays an important part.

- Before reading the poem, show 'Mouse' to the children and discuss the shape of the text together. What might the poem be about? Why do the children think this?

- Read 'Mouse' with the children, pointing to the text during reading following the words down the page. Did they guess correctly what the poem is about? Why do they think the text is written in this particular way? Does it help them to imagine the mouse more easily?

- Ask the children what makes this poem different from others they have explored and whether they like this form of poetry. Encourage them to give reasons for their answers. Respect and value all the opinions that are offered.

- Before reading 'Bananas', show the poem to the children and discuss the shape of the text. What might this poem be about? Encourage them to give you reasons for their opinions. Write their responses on the board.

- Read 'Bananas' to the children. Do they think this poem is different from other poems? Do they think it is different from 'Mouse'? Encourage them to tell you how it is different. Write their answers on the board and compare them with the answers for 'Mouse'.

- Write 'calligram' on the board and read it to the children. (Leave the word on the board while working on these lessons.) Explain to them that this is the term used when the formation of the letters or text in a poem, or the font, help to show the meaning of the poem. For example, jagged letters could be used in a poem about something frightening. Alternatively, letters can be used in the design of a poem. Ask the children to suggest other things that might make good calligrams. List their ideas, using the special style of writing.

With the lower-achievers

With adult support

Choose from:

1   Look again at 'Mouse' and ask the children why they think this poem is a good example of a calligram. Do they remember what a calligram is? Explore again together the shape of the poem and how its text follows the shape of the mouse's tail and so illustrates the poem's subject matter. Do the same with 'Bananas'. Challenge the children to tell you other animals and fruit that might make good subjects for calligrams. Together choose one suggestion and help them to write a poem. (Remind them that it doesn't have to rhyme.)

2   Using Resource sheet 4a, ask the children to complete the shape poem 'Grapes' choosing appropriate words from the words in the boxes. Give reading support if necessary. Let them make up silly ones if they want to!

3   Look at Resource sheet 4b together. Discuss the shape and the words around it. What other words could be used to write a poem inside the shape? Help the children to write a poem. Suggest that they write the words so that they look furry like a rabbit. (Remind them that the poem doesn't have to rhyme.)

Teacher-independent activities

Choose from:

1   Before starting the children off on this task, give them a couple of examples. Ask them to think about how to write the following words to make them calligrams (as on Resource sheet 4c): cold (could have icicles), hot (steamy), tired (droopy letters), funny (letters with smiley faces on them) and sad (letters with tears). They should choose one or more of these words and write them in the style suggested.

2   Let the children complete Resource sheet 4a.

3   Ask the children to work in pairs and look through poetry anthologies for shape poems or calligrams. They should make a table display of these, with the books open at the pages with calligrams. Ask them to write labels for their displays, remembering to use the word 'calligram'. (They will find it on the board from the whole-class session.)

4   Working in pairs, let the children complete Resource sheet 4b. Tell them to make the words they write inside the rabbit look furry like a rabbit.

Plenary session

- Look again at the word 'calligram'. Ask for a volunteer to read it. Challenge the children to tell you what it means.

- Ask the children who looked through the anthologies to share with the class the calligrams they found. Read one or two of these, showing the text to the children.

- Do the children prefer calligrams to conventional poems? Why or why not? Which calligram is their favourite? Why?

Lesson Two

Chosen poems

'The Night-Time Monster' by Frances Mackay, (page 30)

'Sheep' by Collette Drifte, (page 30)

Intended learning

- To explore more shape poems.
- To reinforce the term 'calligram'.
- To use the shape poems as a stimulus for writing own shape poems.

With the whole class

- Enlarge copies of 'The Night-Time Monster' and 'Sheep'.

- Remind the children of the work they did on shape poems previously and the new word that they learned (calligram). Ask for a volunteer to remind you of the word. Who knows what it means? Write it on the board.

- Look at 'The Night-Time Monster' and discuss the shape of the words. Encourage the children to tell you what they think the poem might be about and why they think this.

- Read 'The Night-Time Monster' with the children, pointing to the text. Ask them which words in the poem illustrate their meanings. Point to words such as 'tall', 'fat', 'bed' and 'eyes'. How do these words help to make the calligram?

- Were they right in their guess about the poem's subject matter? How did the shape of the words help them to judge this?

- Look at 'Sheep' and together discuss its shape. What do they think this poem might be about and why do they think so?

- Read 'Sheep' with the children, letting them see the text. Ask them which words in this poem illustrate their meanings. Agree that all the words have curly bits to illustrate a sheep's wool.

With the lower-achievers

With adult support

Choose from:

1 Look again at 'The Night-Time Monster'. Challenge the children to find words other than those in the whole-class session that are good examples for the calligrams. Point out 'hairy', 'jumps', 'monsters' and 'fright'. Ask the children why these are good words for the calligram. Ask them to think of some other frightening words that would be good for calligrams. Write some of their ideas in scary letter shapes.

2 Look again at 'Sheep'. Ask the children what other animal shapes would be good for writing calligrams. Some ideas might be a snake (snake-like letters), a hedgehog (spiky letters), a crocodile (scaly letters), a bird (feathery letters)or a cat (furry letters). Let them choose one and write the name of the animal using those types of letters. They could even try writing a poem.

3 Suggest writing poems with themes that can be illustrated with other media, for example a poem about the beach could have the word 'sand' written in glue with sand stuck on or 'pebbles' written using small stones; a poem about vegetables could have the appropriate words written in dried pulses such as peas, lentils, beans and pearl barley. Help the children to write a poem like this.

4 Give the children copies of Resource sheet 4c. They should complete the poem using the words suggested by making them look like their meanings. Give support where necessary.

Teacher-independent activities

Choose from:

1 Let the children complete Resource sheet 4c. You may need to give them guidance before letting them complete it independently.

2 Let the children work in pairs to practise reciting one of the calligrams. Challenge them to use their bodies to show 'physical calligrams'. For example, if they choose 'Bananas', they could stand in a banana shape while reciting it.

3 Ask the children to use coloured pens to write the names of colours – using a green pen to write 'green', a blue pen to write 'blue' and so on. Explain that while the words are not poems, they also are calligrams.

Plenary session

■ Ask the children who wrote calligrams on resource sheets to share these with the class.

■ Ask the children what 'calligram' means.

■ Ask the children who practised reciting one of the chosen calligrams to give a class performance. Encourage them to show how they devised a 'physical calligram'.

■ Which part of this work did the children enjoy particularly? Encourage them to give reasons for their answers.

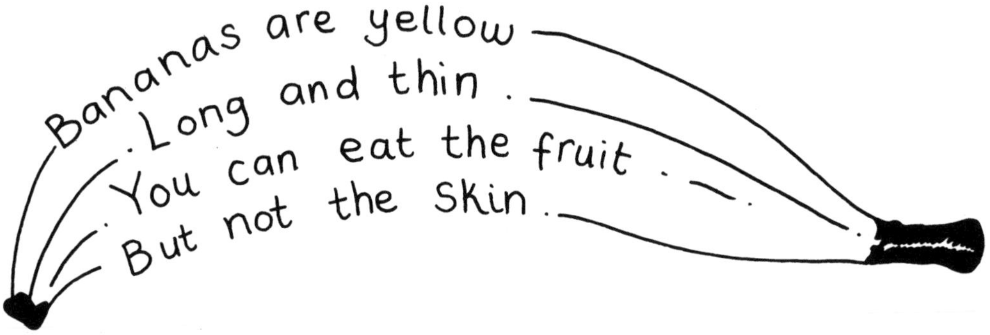

Bananas are yellow
Long and thin .
You can eat the fruit
But not the skin .

Did you know that the mouse's tail is so very long and thin that when the mouse is out the door his tail is still in ?

Sheep are white
and fluffy
Eating grass all day
Making wool
for jumpers
They don't have time to play

TALL, fat and very hairy
The night - time monster is ever so SCARY
He lurks beneath my bed at night
And jumps out suddenly to give me a FRIGHT
But I know the Monster's inside my head
So I close my eyes and snuggle down in bed

■ Finish the poem 'Grapes' by choosing words from the boxes.

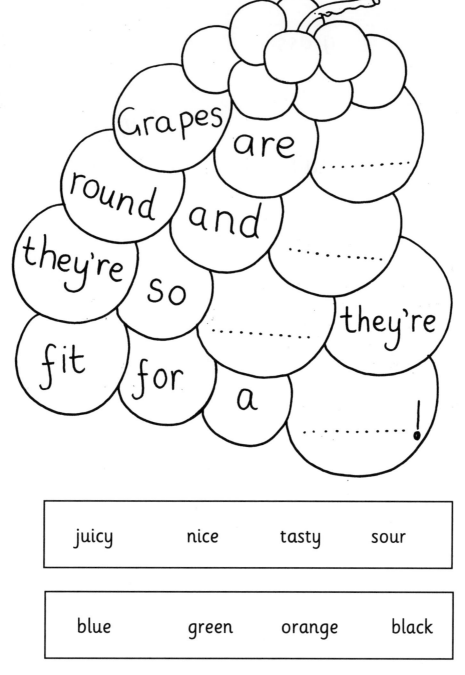

juicy	nice	tasty	sour

blue	green	orange	black

yummy	nice	horrible	great

cat	king	horse	queen

■ Look at this shape. Read the words around it.

grass

rabbit

fluffy

tail

nose

long

white

twitch

ears

■ Write a poem inside the shape. Use the words to help you.

■ Look at these words. They have been written to look like their meaning.

■ Complete this poem rewriting the words in the boxes, making them look like their meaning. Add your words to the poem.

A _____ ladybird fluttered by. | tiny |

Her wings were black and _____ | red |

She rested on a wobbly _____ | leaf |

And settled down to _____ | bed |

■ Now try and write your own calligram on the back of this sheet.

Rhyming and non-rhyming poems

Overall aims

- To distinguish between rhyming and non-rhyming poetry.
- To explore the chosen poems in terms of rhyming and non-rhyming.
- To use the poetry as a basis for own work.

Lesson One

This lesson may take more than one session to complete.

Chosen poems

'Why is it?' by Max Fatchen, (page 37)

'If your hands get wet' by Michael Rosen, (page 37)

Intended learning

- To explore the chosen poems in terms of rhyming and non-rhyming.
- To distinguish between rhyming and non-rhyming poetry.

With the whole class

- Enlarge the poems 'Why is it?' and 'If your hands get wet' and show them to the children. Look at the structure of each poem. Ask if any of the children know what a verse is. How many verses does each poem have?

- Read 'Why is it?' to the children, letting them follow the text. Ask them to tell you what the poem is about, ensuring that they understand its 'plot'. Encourage them to tell similar stories about 'bathroom traffic jams' in their houses. Do they think the poem is funny? Why?

- Remind the children of the work they did about rhyme in Years 1 and 2. Ask them for some of the rhyming words from 'Why is it?' and write them on the board. They should identify 'dirtiest', 'strongest', 'longest'; 'be', 'me'; 'fret', 'wet'; 'cries', 'eyes'; 'howls', 'towels'; 'steaming', 'dreaming'; 'showing', 'flowing'; 'say' and 'stay'. Leave the words on the board.

- Read 'If your hands get wet', letting the children follow the text. Ask them what the poem is about. Does anybody have a similar story to tell about an itch that couldn't be scratched? What things does the poet describe that stop people from scratching their noses? Encourage the children to think of other things. List their ideas on the board.

- Ask the children if they think the poem is funny and encourage them to give reasons for their answers. Ask them to identify any rhyming words in the poem. Are they surprised that they can't? Did they know that poems don't have to rhyme?

- Ask the children which their favourite poem is and why. Do they prefer poems that rhyme to non-rhyming poems? Do they think that rhymes make a difference? Give them the opportunity to explain their answers.

With the lower-achievers

With adult support

Choose from:

1. Read 'Why is it?' once more, encouraging the children to join in. Ask them whether this is a poem that rhymes and how they know. Ask them to name some of the rhyming words. If necessary, look again at the list on the board from the whole-class session and help them to identify the same words on the enlarged copy of the poem. Give each child a copy of Generic sheet 6 (page 118) and help them to write pairs of rhyming words from the poem.

2. Read 'If your hands get wet' again with the children, encouraging them to join in. Is this a poem with or without rhyme? Ask them to say whether they think the poem is funny and why. Does it matter that the poem doesn't rhyme? Why? Do they know any other poems that don't rhyme? Look together in anthologies to find some.

3. Using Resource sheet 5a, help the children to answer the questions and complete the sentences. Give reading support if necessary.

4. Help the children to complete Resource sheet 5b.

Teacher-independent activities

Choose from:

1   Let the children complete Resource sheet 5a, working in pairs if necessary.

2   Ask the children to find one or two other rhyming poems and look for the rhyming words. Give them a copy of Generic sheet 6 (p118) and ask them to write the rhyming words they find.

3   Ask the children to work in pairs and choose their favourite poem. Ask each child to choose their favourite line and practise reciting it, so that each pair will recite two lines. Encourage them to use tone of voice, facial expressions and volume to help express their line's mood.

4   Give the children copies of Resource sheet 5b to complete.

Plenary session

■   Ask for a volunteer to tell you which poem rhymes and which does not. Ask for different volunteers to define 'rhyme'.

■   Ask the children who learned lines from one of the poems to give a class performance. Why did they choose their lines?

■   Ask the children who completed the resource sheets to explain to the others what they did. Those who wrote rhyming words on Generic sheet 6 could read them out to the class. As a class, try to write a different poem using some of those rhyming words.

■   Do the children think that poetry can be fun both with and without rhymes? Why do they think so?

Lesson Two

This lesson may take more than one session to complete.

Chosen poems

'Why is it?' by Max Fatchen, (page 37)

'If your hands get wet' by Michael Rosen, (page 37)

Intended learning

■   To revisit the chosen poems.

■   To use the poetry as a basis for own work.

With the whole class

■   Read the two poems again, putting as much expression into the reading as you can. Let the children see the text and encourage them to join in. Ask them to remind you what the difference between the two is (rhyming and non-rhyming).

■   Explore 'Why is it?' in more detail together. Some of the following ideas can be discussed: there are three verses in the poem (or four, if the final single line is counted as a verse), all with a different number of lines; the rhyming pattern of the poem is not regular but it is obvious; the title of the poem is reflected in the opening line of each verse, although even that is different each time; the poem contains many questions – are they supposed to be answered?

■   Explore 'If your hands get wet' in more detail. Some of the following ideas can be discussed: there are two verses in the poem, one longer than the other; not every line begins with a capital letter; it contains one question in the middle of the poem – is it supposed to be answered?; some final words are repeated such as 'nose' and 'it', but the poem does not rhyme; the poem is written as though the poet is speaking to the reader, with the use of 'you' throughout.

■   Work together to plan a class poem. Ask the children for subject ideas. You could start them off with a few such as 'Bedtime', 'A Sore Finger' or 'Temper Tantrums'. Decide on a subject and brainstorm suitable words and phrases. List them on the board. Decide whether the poem will rhyme – the children may change their minds about this later. Finalise a short poem and write it on a large sheet of paper. Leave it up while doing this lesson. Tell the children they will have the opportunity to write their own poems in their groups.

With the lower-achievers

With adult support

Choose from:

1   Work with the children to write their own rhyming poem about bedtime. Discuss with them what happens at bedtime. Some of the following ideas could be explored: the children always seem to be playing when called in at bedtime; there's usually an argument with Mum or Dad about going to bed; older siblings may stay up later – is this fair and does it cause more trouble?; bedtime stories or reading books may be part of the routine. What rhyming words are associated with bedtime? Make a list. (You could refer to the words in the boxes on Resource sheet 5c to stimulate their ideas.) Write any phrases that they suggest. Help them to write a line or two that they can use in their poems.

2   Using Resource sheet 5c, help the children to complete the rhyming poem about bedtime. There are rhyming words at the bottom of the sheet to help them.

3   Working closely with the children, choose a subject for a non-rhyming poem. Help them to write their own poem. Again, make lists of words or phrases associated with the subject.

Teacher-independent activities

Choose from:

1   Give the children copies of Resource sheet 5c to complete.

2   Ask the children to work in pairs to look through one or two anthologies for examples of both rhyming and non-rhyming poetry. Ask them to choose one of each and mark the pages

with a bookmark. The poems will be read out in the plenary session.

Plenary session

■   Ask the children who chose two poems to show the anthologies to the class. Read the poems they chose, using as much expression as possible. Ask the children which poem rhymes and which doesn't.

■   Let some of the children who completed Resource sheet 5c read out their poems to the class.

■   What have the children learned about rhyming and non-rhyming poetry? Do rhymes make a difference? Why or why not? Which do they prefer? Why?

Why is it?

Why is it,
That,
In our bathroom,
It's not the dirtiest
Or the strongest
Who stays the longest?
BUT
It always seems to be
The one who gets there
Just ahead
Of me.

Why is it
That people fret
When they're wet,
With loud cries
And soap in their eyes
And agonized howls,
Because they forget
Their towels?

Why is it that –
When I'm in the bath,
Steaming and dreaming,
My toes just showing
And the hot water flowing,
That other people
Yell and say,
'Are you there to stay
Or just on a visit?'

Why is it?

Max Fatchen

If your hands get wet

If your hands get wet
in the washing-up water,
if they get covered in flour
if you get grease or oil
all over your fingers
if they land up in the mud,
wet grit, paint, or glue ...

have you noticed
it's just then
that you always get
a terrible itch
just inside your nose?
and you can try and twitch
your nose,
twist your nose,
squeeze your nose
scratch it with your arm
scrape your nose on your
shoulder
or press it up against the wall
but it's no good.
You can't get rid of the itch.
It drives you so mad
you just have to let a finger
    get at it.
And before you know you've
    done it,
you've wiped a load of glue,
or oil,
or cold wet pastry
all over the end of your nose.

Michael Rosen

Name _____

■ Read 'Why is it?' and 'If your hands get wet'.

■ Answer these questions.

Which poem rhymes?

_____

Which poem does not rhyme?

_____

■ Now complete these sentences. (The words at the bottom of the page will help you.)

There are _____ verses in 'Why is it?' and two _____ in 'If your hands get wet'.

'Why is it?' _____ but 'If your hands get wet' does not rhyme.

_____ don't always have to _____

| rhyme | poems | verses | three | rhymes |

■ Write your favourite line from 'Why is it?'

_____

■ Write your favourite line from 'If your hands get wet'.

_____

■ Which is your favourite poem?

_____

■ Why? (The words below might help you.)

_____

laugh	silly	sick	true
yuck	funny	horrible	like
soap	fair	makes	because

■ Complete this rhyming poem about bedtime. You can use the rhyming words in the boxes. You don't have to use all the lines.

Bedtime

Every night at eight _____

It always comes as a bit of a _____

My mother says, "It's time for _____

So up those stairs we slowly _____

And then we _____

_____

_____

bed		go		o'clock
said		no		shock

	play		instead
	stay		tread

cry
why

■ On the back of this sheet, draw a picture to go with your poem.

Stories for openings

Overall aims

- To explore the openings of stories and chapters.

- To understand and use the term 'adjective' appropriately.

- To understand and use the terms 'singular' and 'plural' appropriately.

Featured book

The Thing-on-Two-Legs by Diana Hendry and Sue Heap (Jets/Collins, 1995)

Story synopsis

Mulligan the dog was very happy until the Thing-in-a-Box (Seamus) got out of its box and became the Thing-on-Two-Legs. It began to walk – but so slowly that Mulligan's own lovely long walks with Mr and Mrs Dembo became a thing of the past. Suffering from total frustration and pent-up energy, Mulligan eventually attached himself to Mr Linden and Gary. He went with them to the woods where he had a wonderful time. When Mr Linden took Mulligan home, he found Mrs Dembo very upset because he was missing. When all was explained, a very pleasing agreement was reached: Mr Linden would exercise Mulligan with Gary, in exchange for visiting Seamus now and again. This suited Mulligan down to the ground and he became a very happy dog once more!

Lesson One

Intended learning

- To explore the openings of stories and chapters.

- To use the featured book as a basis for looking at story and chapter openings.

- To look at the openings in other texts.

With the whole class

- Have ready several examples of stories with different openings such as 'Once upon a time', 'One day', 'There was once', 'Long ago' and so on. Read them to the children. Ask them to tell you what you have read to them. (The beginning of a story or the first words of a story.) Explain that these are called 'openings' and that they set the scene of a story.

- List some of the openings on the board and leave them up. Encourage the children to think of other openings. Add these to the list.

- Tell the children that you want them to listen carefully to the way that *The Thing-on-Two-Legs* opens, both at the beginning of the story as a whole and at each chapter. Read Chapter One and at the end, ask the children to remember its opening. Write 'One morning' on the board or, if any of the children can, ask them to write it. Look at the list written at the beginning of the session. Is this opening there?

- Continue reading the book, asking only at the end of a chapter how it opened. Add each opening to the list on the board and leave it up.

- Discuss these openings with the children. Which ones could be used for the opening of any story? Which could be used only in *The Thing-on-Two-Legs* (because there is a reference to one of the characters or the setting)?

- Why do the chapters open as they do? Explain to them that in this book they link the new chapter with the end of the previous one. Look at the endings of some chapters and then the openings of the next ones. Do the children know of any other books like this?

- Look at the list of openings on the board again. Which openings in the list are old-fashioned? (For example, 'Once upon a time' or 'A long time ago'.) Where are these openings likely to be found? (In fairytales or classic stories written years ago.)

With the lower-achievers

With adult support

Choose from:

1 Look again at the opening of each chapter of *The Thing-on-Two-Legs*. Contrast the 'neutral' opening of Chapter One, ('One morning') and the rest of the openings. Can the children remember why the chapters open in this way? Remind them that the opening of each chapter is to link it with the end of the previous one.

Help the children to list two or three endings of one chapter and openings of the next from *The Thing-on-Two-Legs*. Help the children to see the links.

2   Look at other texts, traditional and modern, and discuss their openings. Highlight the less obvious openings to show the children that stories do not have to start with 'Once', 'One day' and so on. Challenge the children to distinguish between modern texts and older ones from the openings.

3   Give the children copies of Resource sheet 6a. They have to match the chapter endings with the next chapter openings. They could then take one of the stories and finish it verbally.

4   Give out copies of Generic sheet 7 (page 119). Read the openings with the children and help them to complete a sentence for each one.

Teacher-independent activities

Choose from:

1   Give the children copies of Resource sheet 6a to complete. They could draw pictures of the endings of the stories on the reverse of the sheet. Alternatively, you could cut out the individual cards and let them play a matching game with them. Which ones don't make sense when put together?

2   Ask the children to work in pairs with copies of Generic sheet 7 (page 119). They should look at the openings and together decide how each sentence could finish. If writing is too difficult, they could record their sentences on a cassette recorder.

3   Photocopy Generic sheet 7 (page 119) onto card and cut out each opening phrase card. Put the cards into a box or bag. Ask the children to work in pairs to make a 'lucky dip' into the box to choose a card. The child who has chosen the card should read it out and challenge their partner to complete the sentence.

Plenary session

■   Has anybody discovered new openings to stories or chapters? Encourage the children to add them to the list using a different colour.

■   Ask the children who completed Generic sheet 7 to either read their completed sentences or play the recording. Encourage the others to suggest alternative endings. (Make sure the children understand that there is no 'right' answer and that all their suggestions are valid.)

■   Do they think the opening of a story is important? Why?

Lesson Two

Intended learning

■   To understand and use the term 'adjective' appropriately.

■   To use the text to explore and identify adjectives.

With the whole class

■   Write some adjectives on the board – for example, 'old', 'red', 'funny', 'thin' and so on. Ask the children to read them. Challenge them to add a noun to each word. For example, 'an old man', 'the red balloon', 'a funny joke' and 'the thin dog'. Ask them to tell you what the original words are doing (describing something). Do they know the correct term? Write 'adjective' on the board.

■   Ask some of the children to come up and write their own examples of adjectives. Display their list while working on this lesson. Ask them to add some nouns to their adjectives. Explain that adjectives usually come before a noun.

■   Look at the first chapter of *The Thing-on-Two-Legs* for adjectives. Discuss examples such as 'hairless', 'decorative', 'useless', 'wonderful' and 'chewable'. Encourage suggestions of other nouns to go with each of these adjectives. Let the children write these on the board themselves.

■   Look again at the original adjectives and ask whether anybody can put them with a verb. Start them off with, for example, '(The man) feels old,' or '(The boy) looks funny.' Explain that adjectives usually come after verbs such as 'be', 'get', 'seem', 'feel' and 'look'. Challenge the children to add verbs to the adjectives and nouns they suggested.

With the lower-achievers

With adult support

Choose from:

1   Look at some of the adjectives from *The Thing-on-Two-Legs*. Ask the children to suggest some nouns to go with two or three of these. Together, decide a sentence for each noun and adjective. Remind the children that the adjective goes before the noun. Do the same for adjectives and verbs, reminding the children that the adjective goes after the verb.

2   Using Resource sheet 6b, help the children to identify the adjectives and circle them in red. Give reading support if necessary. Help them to write a sentence for two or three of these.

3   Using Generic sheet 8 (page 120), help the children to match an adjective and a noun and/or a verb and an adjective. They could use some from the whole-class session or make up some of their own. (You can use other adjectives by blanking out the given adjectives on this sheet and replacing them with others of your choice.)

4   Work with Generic sheet 9 (page 121) as a group. Talk about the picture and discuss all the different adjectives to be found. Write out those that the children find. Alternatively, match the adjectives to some word cards made earlier. Can they find other adjectives for which you haven't made a card?

Teacher-independent activities

Choose from:

1   Make cards with adjectives written on some, nouns written on others and verbs on a third set. Place them face down in their separate piles and ask the children to work in pairs or groups of three. They should take a card from each pile and make a sentence from the three cards. If writing the sentences is difficult, they could record them onto a cassette.

2   Give the children copies of Resource sheet 6b to complete.

3   Give the children copies of Generic sheet 9 (page 121). Ask them to work in pairs to identify the different adjectives illustrated. Ask them to try to write some of them down or match them to adjective cards.

Plenary session

■   Ask the children what an adjective does. Do they remember where an adjective usually comes, relative to a noun and a verb? Ask for volunteers to come to the board and write some examples of adjectives.

■   Play a game where you name an object that can be seen in the room and the children have to suggest adjectives for that object. For example, you say *"door"* and the children could say *"green"* or you say *"table"* and the children say *"flat"*. Challenge them to some up with some more interesting adjectives.

Lesson Three

Intended learning

■   To understand and use the terms 'singular' and 'plural' appropriately.

■   To use the text to explore and identify singulars and plurals.

With the whole class

■   Write on the board a list of singular nouns – for example, 'dog', 'coat', 'girl', 'car' and 'house'. (Make sure they are nouns with regular plurals.) Ask for volunteers to read them and tell you how many of each there are. How do they know? Ask for children to come and write a singular noun on the board themselves.

■   Write 'singular' on the board, read it with the children and explain that this is the term we use when talking about one of anything. Ask them to tell you the term for 'more than one'.

- Write 'plural' on the board, read it with the children and explain (if necessary) what it means. Encourage them to tell you the plurals of the nouns already on the board. Challenge them to come and write the plurals. Ask the class what was added to make the plurals. If necessary, show them how these plurals have 's' at the end.

- Explain that some plurals are different:
  – they may end in 'es' (such as 'kisses', 'guesses' and 'loaves')

  – they may be irregular (such as 'mouse/mice', 'person/people' and 'child/children')

  – they may be the same, whether singular or plural (such as 'sheep' and 'deer').

  Ask if anyone can give you more examples of each type. List their suggestions and leave them on the board for referring to later. (Collective nouns are explored in Chapter 7.)

With the lower-achievers

With adult support

Choose from:

1 Look for singular nouns in *The Thing-on-Two-Legs*. Together, list them on a large sheet of paper. Discuss the examples you have found, agree what the plurals of these would be and write these next to the singular nouns. Then discuss whether the plurals are regular or irregular.

2 Using Resource sheet 6c, ask the children to make the singulars into plurals and vice versa. They should then read the words beside the boxes and draw the pictures.

3 Use a set of noun cards and play a game of 'Singular and Plural'. Place the cards face down on the table and ask each child to turn one over. Ask them to tell you the plural of the noun in the picture. If they are correct, they may keep the card. The winner has the highest number of cards at the end of the game.

4 Prepare Generic sheet 10 (page 122) by writing in the hot-air balloons a variety of singular nouns which have irregular plurals. Help the children to write the plurals in the baskets.

Teacher-independent activities

Choose from:

1 Give the children copies of Resource sheet 6c to complete.

2 Give the children copies of Generic sheet 9 (page 121). Ask them to identify things that they can only see one of (single) and things they can see more than one of (plural). They should circle the single things in one colour and the plurals in another. Challenge them to write some of the words on another sheet of paper.

3 Give the children copies of Generic sheet 6 (page 118) with some nouns written in the left-hand boxes (use those that you are happy are not too difficult for them). They have to use dictionaries to find the plurals and write them in the opposite boxes.

Plenary session

- Let the children who completed resource sheets or made cassette recordings share with the class what they did. Ask a volunteer from the group to explain their task and what they found.

- Ask for a volunteer to write on the board an example of an irregular plural together with its singular. In what way is it an irregular plural?

- Write on the board 'singular' and 'plural'. Ask for volunteers to tell you what they say and what they mean.

Name _____

■ Match the chapter endings with the next chapter openings.

The tiny mouse looked into the eyes of a very big cat.

John woke up and remembered his dream.

The teacher told Max and his sister that they were in big trouble!

But he wasn't afraid,

Just when he thought he was safe a huge elephant fell on top of him!

Suddenly, Iqbal had an idea.

How were they going to escape from the island?

When their parents heard about it,

Name _____

■ Draw a red circle around the adjectives. (There are six of them.)

pretty   cat   yellow

want   big   no

yes   thin   said

pen   funny   dog

smelly   house   jump

■ Write sentences for three of the adjectives.

_____

_____

_____

Name _____

■ Write the plurals of these words.

bed _____   apple _____

cat _____   gate _____

house _____   flower _____

■ Write these words in the singular.

cars _____   books _____

shoes _____   boys _____

doors _____   bananas _____

■ Draw pictures in the boxes.

cups

dog

star

forks

Stories for endings

Overall aims

- To explore the endings of traditional stories.
- To invent alternative endings to traditional stories.
- To understand and use appropriately the term 'collective noun'.
- To correctly use the apostrophe for contraction.

Featured books

Cinderella, Jack and the Beanstalk, Little Red Riding Hood

No specific edition is recommended. Teachers should select the edition most appropriate for their needs. If other traditional tales are preferred, the lesson plans can be easily adapted to use them.

Lesson One

Intended learning

- To explore the endings of traditional stories.
- To invent alternative endings to traditional stories.
- To discuss the endings of other texts with a view to suggesting alternatives.

With the whole class

- Ask if anyone can remember the story of Cinderella. If so, ask the child to retell it and then read the chosen version of the story. When you have finished, ask the children to retell the ending of the story.

- Explain that this is the traditional ending of the tale but now you want them to think of a different ending. Give them a start by suggesting that when the prince brings the glass slipper for Cinderella to try on, it does not fit. Ask the children to continue this new version. Some ideas might include: the slipper fitting one of the ugly sisters who then marries the prince, making Cinderella's life worse than ever; Cinderella discovering that the prince is not really a prince but that he was also helped by a fairy godmother – they marry but continue to

live in poverty; the prince going off to find the owner of the slipper, failing and eventually returning for Cinderella who, in the meantime, has married his brother.

- Read the chosen version of *Jack and the Beanstalk*. Encourage the children to suggest alternative endings. Discuss some of the following ideas: Jack makes friends with the giant and decides to stay, to avoid returning to his nagging mother; Jack fails to kill the giant, who manages to climb to the bottom of the beanstalk and kill both Jack and his mother; the giant comes to Jack's house, falls in love with Jack's mother and they marry and live happily ever after.

- Do the children like making alternative endings? Encourage them to say why/why not. Do they think the traditional endings should be left alone? Why? Ask them if they find it difficult to make up the new endings.

With the lower-achievers

With adult support

Choose from:

1 Revisit the alternative endings of *Cinderella* and *Jack and the Beanstalk* that were suggested in the whole-class session. Discuss which ending is the children's favourite and why. Decide on one of these and help them to make a book with the new ending. Ask the children to illustrate the new story.

2 Read the chosen version of *Little Red Riding Hood*. Work with the children to invent alternative endings. These might include: the wolf becoming tame and living with Grandma as her pet; Little Red Riding Hood deciding she isn't going to visit Grandma any more and running away; the wood-cutter refusing to kill the wolf and leaving Little Red Riding Hood to sort out her own problems. Help the children to write their new endings.

3 Using Resource sheet 7a, help the children to write alternative endings to the illustrated fairytales. They could use the ideas at the bottom of the sheet or make up their own.

Teacher-independent activities

Choose from:

1 Ask the children to choose their favourite alternative ending for *Jack and the Beanstalk* and draw a large picture to illustrate this. They should write a caption at the bottom of their picture.

2 Give the children copies of Resource sheet 7a to complete. Tell them to use dictionaries to help them write the words.

3 Ask the children to work in pairs to decide on an alternative ending to one of the fairytales. They should record this onto a cassette or, if possible, write a few words.

Plenary session

■ Has anybody made up a new ending that is totally different from those discussed in the whole-class session? Encourage the children to share their version with the others.

■ Do the children think the ending of a story is important? Encourage them to tell you how and why. Do they prefer happy endings? Does it matter if some of the characters don't live happily ever after? Why?

Lesson Two
. . . .

Intended learning

■ To understand and use appropriately the term 'collective noun'.

■ To use texts to find examples of collective nouns.

With the whole class

■ Remind the children of the work they did on nouns. Do any of them remember what a noun is? Ask for volunteers to come and write some nouns on the board. Then ask if any of the children can write the plurals as well.

■ Tell the children that they are now going to learn about a special type of noun called a 'collective noun'. Explain what it is. Encourage the children to give you some examples of collective nouns – for example, they might be in a 'class', a 'group', a 'team' or a 'house'.

■ Do they know of any other collective nouns? Give them a start, if necessary, by suggesting a 'bunch' of flowers, a 'herd' of cows, a 'pile' of newspapers or a 'flock' of sheep. Write on the board any of their suggestions or let them write their ideas themselves.

■ Look through the selected texts of fairytales asking the children to listen for collective nouns – for example, the 'family' of bears (Goldilocks) or a 'forest' of pine trees (Hansel and Gretel).

■ Point out to the children that these collective nouns are written in the singular (without a final 's') even though they refer to several items in a group. Ask them to tell you what you would mean if you spoke of 'bunches of flowers' or 'herds of cows'.

With the lower-achievers

With adult support

Choose from:

1 Make sure that the children fully understand what collective nouns are. If necessary, discuss them together again until they have grasped the idea. Together, make a chart with as many collective nouns as possible, such as a 'bunch' of keys, a 'litter' of puppies and a 'group' of people. Write the examples in different colours. Use a simple dictionary and look each one up.

2 Using Resource sheet 7b, help the children to match the collective nouns to the pictures. Ask them to write a sentence for one or two of the examples on the back of the sheet.

3 Work with the children to make up some new collective nouns, for example a 'bundle' of pencils, a 'bathload' of soap and a 'gurgle' of babies. Ask them to illustrate their collective nouns.

Teacher-independent activities

Choose from:

1 Give the children copies of Resource sheet 7b to complete. Alternatively, you could cut out the pictures and words and let them play a

matching game with them. For example, with 'Pelmanism', the cut-out cards are placed randomly face down and the children have to turn over two and try to match them, turning them face down again if they are unsuccessful.

2   Prepare two sets of cards, one with collective nouns written on them and one with the objects themselves. For example, on one card would be written 'flock' and on another 'sheep'. Let the children play a game by pairing the sets of cards. They should place the cards face up for the first game. If they are confident, they could turn the cards face down for the next games.

3   Give the children some collective noun cards, such as 'flock' and 'herd'. Ask them to think of other more unusual things to use these words with. This might make silly sentences, such as 'a flock of daffodils' or 'a herd of shoes'. They could illustrate their ideas (flying daffodils and shoes standing in the corner of a field together).

Plenary session

■   Write 'collective nouns' on the board and ask for volunteers to come and write some examples. Has anybody made up new collective nouns? Let them come and write them up, or tell the class while you write them.

■   Ask the children who worked independently to make up some silly collective nouns to tell the class their ideas.

■   Make sure everybody fully understands what collective nouns are.

Lesson Three

Intended learning

■   To understand the term 'apostrophe' and to recognise the symbol.

■   To correctly use the apostrophe for contraction.

With the whole class

■   Write 'Do not' and 'Don't' on the board. Ask for volunteers to read these. What is the difference between the two? Highlight the apostrophe in a different colour and explain what it does. Show the children how it has replaced the 'o' in 'not' and made the two words into one. Write 'apostrophe' on the board and read it with the children. Explain that when the apostrophe makes one word out of two like this, the new word is called a contraction. Write 'contraction' on the board. Read it with the children.

■   Encourage the children to give you examples of other contracted words, such as 'can't', 'won't' and 'haven't'. Write their examples on the board. (Leave the list up for reference during the group session.) Ask them to tell you what the full words are. This is particularly important for irregular and less obvious contractions such as 'won't' for 'will not'.

■   Play a game of 'Contraction Dialogues'. You ask a child a question containing a word that can be contracted in the answer and they should reply with the contraction. For example, 'Hisham, can you fly?' Hisham should reply, 'No, I can't.' Then ask the others what the original words would be: 'can' and 'not'.

With the lower-achievers

With adult support

Choose from:

1   Explore again the examples of contracted words discussed in the whole-class session. Make sure the children fully understand the term 'apostrophe' and what the apostrophe does. Play 'Contraction Dialogues' again to reinforce the

point. Together, make a list of all the contracted words. Make sure the children know what the two original words were in each case. Put the list on the wall (together with a pen on a string) and ask the children to add new examples to it.

2   Using Resource sheet 7c, help the children to contract the examples given, and use the apostrophe for the contraction. They should then match each contraction to the sentences at the bottom of the sheet.

3   Prepare Generic sheet 10 (page 122) with words to be contracted written in the balloons. (You could take them from Resource sheet 7c or from the whole-class session list on the board.) Ask the children to write in the basket what the contracted word should be. Give support if necessary. Alternatively, do it the other way round with contracted words written on the balloons.

4   Give the children a copy of Generic sheet 11 (page 123) and ask them to make word wheels so they can find as many contracted words as they can.

Teacher-independent activities

Choose from:

1   Let the children complete Resource sheet 7c.

2   Prepare Generic sheet 10 (page 122) with a mixture of contracted words and words to be contracted written in the balloons. (You could take them from Resource sheet 7c or from the whole-class session list on the board.) Ask the children to write in the basket the new word or original two words, as appropriate.

3   Give the children Generic sheet 11 (page 123) and ask them to make word wheels before finding as many contracted words as they can.

Plenary session

■   What have the children learned about apostrophes? Encourage them to tell you why the apostrophe is used and what a contracted word is.

■   Do any of the children want to come and write on the board some of the contracted words they found? Make sure they remember to put in the apostrophe. Ask them what the original words were – for example, if they write 'won't', they should know that the original words were 'will not'.

■   Ask for volunteers to share with the class what they did in their group session. Does everybody understand what they did in this lesson? Was there anything difficult?

■ Write new endings to these fairytales. There are some at the bottom of the sheet to help you.

_____
_____
_____
_____

_____
_____
_____
_____

_____
_____
_____
_____

She is cross with the prince and tells him to go away.	The cat runs away and goes to live on a farm.	She spits it out and runs away from the wicked queen.

■ Write the collective nouns under each picture.
  (You will find them at the bottom of the sheet.)

_____   _____

_____   _____

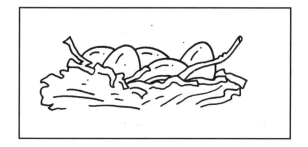

_____   _____

a bunch of flowers	a clutch of eggs
a litter of puppies	a flock of sheep
a pair of shoes	a group of people

■ Use an apostrophe to contract these words.
One has been done for you.

will not _____ **→** _____ won't _____

do not _____ **→** _____

can not _____ **→** _____

is not _____ **→** _____

have not _____ **→** _____

must not _____ **→** _____

■ Now put each word into one of these sentences.

We _____ hit other people.

No! I _____ got to bed.

That _____ fair!

We _____ done our work yet.

I _____ want to eat my dinner.

The boy _____ go out to play today.

Stories for main points

Overall aims

- To use the chosen text to explore the main points of a story.
- To plan the main points of own story before writing it.
- To recognise and understand the singular and plural personal pronouns.
- To practise 'Look, Say, Cover, Write, Check' as a strategy for learning spellings.

Featured book

Omnibombulator by Dick King-Smith (Young Corgi, 1996)

Story synopsis

Omnibombulator was given his long, impressive name because he is such a tiny beetle, and his parents wanted him to feel important. Unfortunately, nobody else feels that Omnibombulator is important and he is pushed around and walked on by the other creepy-crawlies. One day, Omnibombulator decides to see the world and soon finds that there are distinct advantages to being so small, particularly when smelly toes and magpies are around, not to mention a beautiful, very small, lady beetle!

Lesson One

Intended learning

- To use the chosen text to explore the main points of a story.
- To plan the main points of own story before writing it.

With the whole class

- Show *Omnibombulator* to the children and discuss its cover. Encourage them to guess from the cover what the story might be about.
- Challenge the children to tell you what exactly a 'story' is. Explain to them that all stories have main points to them that the author planned

before he or she wrote the book. Ask them to suggest why an author would plan the main points of a story before he or she started to write. What are the advantages of planning a story first? Point out that when we plan the main points of a story, we write a few words that we add to later.

- Read *Omnibombulator* to the children, showing them the text and, particularly, the illustrations. At key points in the story, pause and discuss these with the children. Write key words about the main points on the board as you reach them and discuss these key words as well. Leave these written on the board.

- At the end of the book, ask the children what the main points of the story were. Discuss some of the following. Why was Omnibombulator given his name? How did this fail? What tactics did he adopt to make others take notice of him? Why did he decide to seek his fortune? What adventures did he have? Why did he realise that home is best? How did he manage to turn being tiny to his advantage in the end?

- Look again at the key words that you wrote while reading *Omnibombulator*. Were all the main points of the story identified by the children? Ask them to tell you which of these were the most important points and why, for example how Omnibombulator's size seems to be a disadvantage initially but is his trump card.

With the lower-achievers

With adult support

Choose from:

1 Explore again the main points of the story, as discussed in the whole-class session. Make sure that the children grasp the idea of teasing out the principal points of a story. Help them to write out the main points of *Omnibombulator*. They can then illustrate each point.

2 Using another favourite story (preferably one very different from *Omnibombulator*), work with the children to identify its main points. Help them to write out the main points and then illustrate each point.

3 Give the children a story title that is specific in nature, for example 'The Boy/Girl Who Got

Lost in the Snow' or 'Max, the Brave Rescue-Dog'. Work with the children to plan a story based on the title, making a list of the main points. Agree the story, with you scribing. It could be made into a book and illustrated.

4   Using Resource sheet 8a, ask the children to look at the pictures from *Snow White and the Seven Dwarfs* and read the sentences. They should decide which the main points of the story are and match them to the pictures. Give reading support if necessary.

Teacher-independent activities

Choose from:

1   Ask the children to work in pairs. They should choose a well-known story and decide together its main points. Ask them to write a word or two for each main point and then illustrate them.

2   Give the children copies of Resource sheet 8a to complete. You may need to read it with them before sending them off to work independently.

3   Ask the children to work in pairs to plan a story called 'Jim, the Giant who was Scared of Spiders'. The title should be written out for them together with a word bank. They should also use dictionaries. They write a word or two about each main point and then draw a small sketch to illustrate each. They can then either write the story or record it on cassette.

Plenary session

■   Ask the children what they have learned about the craft of writing stories. The key is for the children to mention that in planning, they need to note the main points of the story.

■   Ask the children who wrote their own stories to volunteer to read them. Before they begin, they could briefly outline the main points.

■   Ask the children who wrote 'Jim, the Giant who was Scared of Spiders' to tell their story.

Lesson Two

Intended learning

■   To recognise and understand the singular and plural personal pronouns.

■   To use the featured text as a basis for exploring these.

With the whole class

■   Remind the children of the work they did on singulars and plurals in Chapter 6. Ask them to give you a few quick-fire examples of nouns in both the singular and the plural, just to recap. Explain that people as well as things are singular or plural. Ask for some examples.

■   Write on the board 'I', 'you', 'he', 'she', and 'it' and ask for volunteers to read them. Ask the children to tell you whether these are singular or plural words. How do they know?

■   Write on the board 'we', 'you', 'they' and 'them' and ask some children to read them. Ask the children to tell you whether these words are singular or plural. How do they know? Match the singulars to the plurals. Make a point of 'you' being identical, regardless of number.

■   Ask for volunteers to come to the board and write 's' beside the singular pronouns and 'p' beside the plurals.

■   Play a game of 'True or False Football'. Divide the class into football teams, letting the children choose the club names. Make a statement and ask a child whether it's true or false. For example, *"Manjit, 'we' is singular, true or false?"*; *"Clare, 'I' is plural, true or false?"* and *"Lee-Wei, 'it' is singular, true or false?"* A correct answer scores a goal.

■   Look at some passages from *Omnibombulator* together and ask the children to show you the personal pronouns. List them on the board. If any occur more than once, make a mark beside the original word.

With the lower-achievers

With adult support

Choose from:

1   Make sure the children fully understand the concept of singular and plural personal pronouns. Ask them to give you verbal examples of sentences using these. Remind them that 'you' is used for both singular and plural. Play 'True or False Football' again to reinforce the point if necessary.

2   Using Resource sheet 8b, ask the children to read the pronouns and join each one to 'singular' or 'plural'. They should then complete the wordsearch.

3   Prepare three sets of cards, one with a different personal pronoun written on each card, one with 'singular' written on every card and the third with 'plural' written on every card. Place the 'singular' and 'plural' cards face up and the pronoun cards face down. Play a game where the children have to take a pronoun card, read it and select a matching card from one of the other two piles. If they are correct, they may keep the set.

Teacher-independent activities

Choose from:

1   Make a set of cards with personal pronouns written on them, one set singular and one set plural. On the back of each card write whether the pronoun on the reverse is singular or plural. Shuffle the two sets together and place the pack face up on the table. Put a 'Snakes and Ladders' board on the table and give each child a counter or tiddlywink. The children should take turns to pick up a card, read it, identify it as singular or plural, check whether they are correct by looking at the back of the card and then put the card at the bottom of the pile. If they are correct, they move their counter along the board. When they reach either a snake or a ladder, they go up it. The winner reaches the top first.

2   Using the cards made for activity 1 above, place all the cards in a 'feely bag' and ask the children to work in pairs or groups of three (one bag to each group). They take a card from the 'feely

bag', read it and identify it as singular or plural. They check with the reverse of the card and if they are correct they may keep the card. The winner is the person who has the most cards at the end of the game.

3   Give the children copies of Resource sheet 8b to complete.

Plenary session

■   Does everybody understand which personal pronouns are singular and which are plural? Ask for volunteers to tell you, or write on the board, which are in each category.

■   Ask somebody from the group(s) that played the games to explain to the class how the game(s) worked.

Lesson Three

Intended learning

■   To revise 'Look, Say, Cover, Write, Check' as a strategy for learning spellings.

■   To spell selected words from the featured book in order to practise using the 'Look, Say, Cover, Write, Check' method.

With the whole class

■   Write on the board 'Look, Say, Cover, Write, Check'. Ask for a volunteer to read the words. Do the children know what, together, these words mean? Remind them that it is a strategy for learning spellings. Ask them to tell you how the method works. Ask someone to choose a word from their spelling programme and write it on the board. Together, work through each part of the strategy.

■   Now choose two or three words from *Omnibombulator* and write these on the board. Working with the children, go through the stages of the method, to learn each word. Ask for volunteers to act as 'guinea pigs' for you to demonstrate the method.

- Ask for a volunteer to show you, unaided, how the method works. Let the child come to the board to give a demonstration. (Give positive feedback for having a go, even if you have to correct part of the demonstration!)

- Let the children give you a few words to learn! Show them how the method works by 'learning' the spelling as if it really is new to you.

With the lower-achievers

With adult support

Choose from:

1 Let the children choose some words from their current spelling programme. Work with them on 'Look, Say, Cover, Write, Check' to learn the spellings, using Generic sheet 12 (page 124). Give them plenty of encouragement at each stage of the method.

2 Using Resource sheet 8c, help the children to learn the words from *Omnibombulator*, using 'Look, Say, Cover, Write, Check'. Make sure that the children understand how the method works.

3 Play 'Spelling Races'. Divide the children into two teams. Using the words from Resource sheet 8c and/or words from their spelling programme, ask the children to spell them, using 'Look, Say, Cover, Write, Check'. Award a 'win' for each correct use of the method. The team that reaches a given target first (for example, five correct uses) is the winner. (It is important at this stage to ensure that the method is being followed correctly – total accuracy of spellings can be demanded when the technique has been fully understood.)

Teacher-independent activities

Choose from:

1 Ask the children to learn the spellings from *Omnibombulator* on Resource sheet 8c, using 'Look, Say, Cover, Write, Check'. Ask them to work in pairs and help each other.

2 Prepare Generic sheet 12 (page 124) with spellings from the children's current spelling list. Ask the children to work in pairs to learn

these and check them. Say you will ask them to tell you the correct spellings later (without looking!).

3 Let the children play 'Hangman' using the spellings from their current list.

Plenary session

- Ask for a volunteer to come to the board and give a demonstration of 'Look, Say, Cover, Write, Check'. If necessary, revise the method once more and make sure everybody understands how it works.

- Ask for volunteers who learned how to spell words from resource or generic sheets to spell their words. (Make sure they are applauded for trying – it is important at this stage that the children are introduced to the method in a positive and stress-free way. It is a strategy that they will be using for the rest of their primary school career and they need to feel comfortable with it.)

■ Match the main points of the story to the pictures.

<u>Snow White and the Seven Dwarfs</u>

■ Snow White looked after the Seven Dwarfs.

■ The Wicked Queen thought she was the most beautiful.

■ The Wicked Queen had yellow hair.

■ Snow White went to live with the Seven Dwarfs.

■ Snow White had black hair.

■ Snow White was poisoned with an apple.

■ There were seven dwarfs.

■ The prince took the poisonous apple away from Snow White.

■ Join each pronoun to **singular** or **plural**.

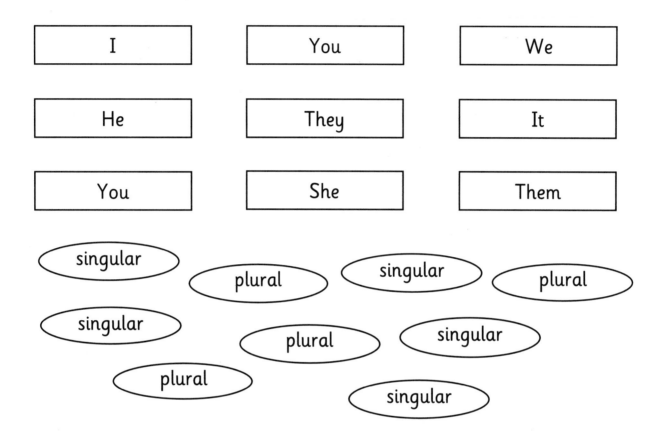

■ Complete the wordsearch. You may go across or down.

i	t	t	h	t
w	s	h	e	h
t	h	e	m	m
w	e	y	o	u
k	w	a	m	I

you
I
we
he
it
she
them
they

■ Follow the numbers.

1 Learn the words at the bottom of the page.

5 Write

_____

_____

_____

_____

_____

6 Check

fold back

2 Look   beetle
garden
birds
boots
small

4 Cover

3 Say

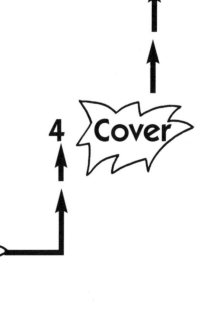

Poems from other cultures

Overall aims

- To explore poems from different cultures.

- To use the poems to compare other cultures with that of Britain.

- To discuss how the alternative culture influences the poetry studied.

Featured book

A Spider Bought a Bicycle and other poems for young children, selected by Michael Rosen (Kingfisher Books, 1992)

Lesson One

Chosen poem

'Eskimo Lullaby' (Anon, Greenland), (page 65)

Intended learning

- To use the chosen poem to stimulate study of Innuit culture.

- To compare Innuit culture with that of Britain.

- To discuss how the poem has been influenced by Innuit culture.

With the whole class

- Enlarge 'Eskimo Lullaby'. Read the title to the children and ask them what they think the poem might be about. Ask the children to tell you what a lullaby is. Do they know who Eskimos are? Explain that the people are more properly called Innuit. Encourage them to use this name. Read the poem to the children, allowing them to follow the text.

- Discuss the poem with the children. For example, do they think the poem was written by a poet living in Britain? Encourage them to explain their answers. Write key words on the board for each of their answers. Some of the following ideas can be discussed: the baby is being carried in the mother's hood (not a buggy or a sling but a hood, probably of a parka); the mother uses the image of a walrus when speaking of the baby's two teeth (not an animal found in Britain); the mother speaks several times of her baby being heavy in the hood, in contrast to a British mother who would not carry her baby around in such a way; in the first two verses the mother says, 'Oh, how heavy he is!' but in the final verse she exclaims, 'Oh I like my baby heavy/And my hood full!', thus showing that, although she finds it difficult to carry her fat baby like this, she actually likes it.

- Tell the children that the poem is from Greenland and that many Innuit live there. Look at an atlas or globe together and find Greenland. Show the distance between Britain and Greenland.

- Ask the children what they know about Innuit culture. Write any key words on the board, such as 'caribou', 'igloo', 'snow', 'seals', 'Arctic' and 'walrus'. Discuss the words and explain the meanings of any they don't know. Leave the words on the board while working on this lesson.

With the lower-achievers

With adult support

Choose from:

1   Read the poem again with the children, encouraging them to join in. Ask them what they think is in the poem that makes it special to Innuit culture. Talk about some of the points that were explored in the whole-class session. Make sure the children understand the meaning of any new words.

2   Look at some books about Innuit culture. Help the children to discover where the Innuit live, in what type of housing, what they eat, how they obtain their food and how they are clothed, transported and entertained. Encourage them to compare Innuit culture with British culture. What is similar and what is different?

3   Using Resource sheet 9a, ask the children to put a tick beside the words that are associated with the Innuit. They should then complete the sentences, using some of the words. Give reading support if necessary.

4   Help the children to learn part (or all) of the poem for a class performance. They could take

one or two lines each and between them recite the whole poem. Encourage them to speak their lines with intonation and expression that helps to put across the atmosphere of the poem.

Teacher-independent activities

Choose from:

1   Ask the children to make a model of an Innuit house or settlement (according to ability) using building bricks, boxes, cubes or other chosen materials. They should write a label or caption for each part of their model. Leave the model and the captions on display while working on this subject.

2   Give the children copies of Resource sheet 9a to complete. You may need to read it with them before letting them work independently.

3   Ask the children to draw a large picture of an igloo and in each 'brick' of snow to write a word that is connected with their Innuit studies. Make a display of these.

4   Prepare a wordsearch using Generic sheet 13 (page 125) with each of the Innuit words discussed in the whole-class session. Let the children do the wordsearch. They could work in pairs to help each other.

Plenary session

■   Ask the children who learned the poem to give a class performance.

■   Has anybody found out something new about the Innuit while exploring books? Ask them to share it with the class.

■   Do the children think the poem captures the idea of an Innuit mother and her baby? Why or why not?

■   Did they enjoy finding out about Innuit culture? What was their favourite part of the lesson?

Lesson Two

Chosen poem

'Sly Mongoose' (Anon, Caribbean), (page 65)

Intended learning

■   To discuss how the poem has been influenced by the Caribbean culture.

■   To use the chosen poem to stimulate a study of the Caribbean culture.

With the whole class

■   Enlarge 'Sly Mongoose'. Read the title of the poem to the children and ask what they think it might be about. Do they know what a mongoose is? Use a dictionary to look up the meaning and show the children a picture of a mongoose from an information book. Read the poem to the children, allowing them to follow the text.

■   Do the children think the poem was written by a poet living in Britain? Why or why not? Tell them that the poem is from the Caribbean and that it is probably a song to be sung while working.

■   Look at an atlas or globe together with the children and find the Caribbean. Show the distance between Britain and the Caribbean. Are there any children in your class who (or whose family) originate from the Caribbean? Do they visit the Caribbean? Ask them to tell one or two things about their family.

■   Explain to the children that native people were captured in Africa and brought to the Caribbean to work as slaves on big plantations, either in the fields or around the homesteads. Look for Africa on a globe or in an atlas and plot the journey from there to the Caribbean. Explain to the children that this was the slave route. The slaves used to sing songs to help them to work and this is why it is likely that the poem was originally a work-song.

■   Discuss the poem together. Do the children know what 'sly' means? How does the reader know that the poem is from the Caribbean? Some of the following ideas can be explored: the dialect used is Caribbean (words such as 'you' for 'your', 'de' for 'the', 'know' used without the final 's', 'pick' used without the final 'ed', 'chicken' used in the singular); the reference to 'de master's kitchen' shows that this is a slave's song, probably a woman who worked in the house; the poem is about a mongoose, which is found in Africa (not native to the Caribbean, or to Britain), so the poem shows how memories of the old country were brought to the plantations by the slaves.

■ If there are Caribbean children in the class, perhaps they could bring from home some things that illustrate Caribbean culture.

With the lower-achievers

With adult support

Choose from:

1   Read the poem again with the children, encouraging them to join in. Ask them what they think is in the poem that makes it special to Caribbean culture. Discuss again the points explored in the whole-class session, making sure they understand any new or unusual words. Do they like the poem? Encourage them to give reasons for their answers and assure them that a negative opinion is as valid as a positive one and has the same right to be respected.

2   Using Resource sheet 9b, ask the children to choose the correct answers to the questions about a mongoose. If necessary, help them to use a simple encyclopedia or other reference book to find out about the mongoose.

3   Working closely with the children, help them to find information about the slave trade and the Caribbean as it was then and as it is now. Together make a book about the Caribbean, illustrated by the children. They should write simple captions, or if possible a sentence or two, for each picture. Leave the book in the class library for the others to read.

4   Using Resource sheet 9c, help the children to complete the wordsearch. They should then read the words at the bottom of the sheet and

write either 'I' for a word associated with the Innuit or 'C' for a word associated with the Caribbean. Give reading support if necessary.

Teacher-independent activities

Choose from:

1   Ask the children to illustrate the poem about the mongoose stealing a chicken and to write a few words or label their picture.

2   Let the children complete Resource sheet 9b. You may need to read it with them before letting them work independently.

3   Ask the children to work in pairs and use an encyclopedia to find 'Caribbean' or 'slaves'. Ask them to find out what they can, referring to a dictionary for words they don't understand.

4   Give the children copies of Resource sheet 9c to complete.

Plenary session

■ Ask the children who researched Caribbean or slaves to tell the others what they found.

■ Do the children think the poem helps them to imagine a slave doing her work in the master's house? Encourage them to give reasons for their answers.

■ Did they enjoy finding out about the Caribbean culture? Was there anything they discovered that they did not like – for example, the idea of slavery?

Eskimo Lullaby

It's my fat baby
I feel in my hood,
Oh, how heavy he is!

When I turn my head
He smiles at me, my baby,
Hidden in my hood,
Oh, how heavy he is!

How pretty he is when he smiles
With his two teeth, like a little walrus!
Oh I like my baby heavy
And my hood full!

Anon (Greenland)

Sly Mongoose

Sly mongoose
Dog know you ways
Sly mongoose
Dog know you ways
Mongoose went to de master's kitchen
Pick up one of de fattest chicken
Put it in de wais'-coat pocket
Sly mongoose

Anon (Caribbean)

■ Tick the words which tell you something about the Innuit.

roses ☐   caribou ☐

sheep ☐   igloo ☐

Arctic ☐   sunshine ☐

Britain ☐   walrus ☐

snow ☐   seals ☐

■ Complete the sentences using some of the words you ticked.

The real name for Eskimos is I_____

They live in the A_____

A snow house is called an i_____

An igloo is made of s_____

Innuit hunt c_____ for food and clothing.

■ Choose the correct words to complete the sentences.

A mongoose is _____

| an animal. |
| a bird. |

It lives in _____

| Africa. |
| Britain. |

Mongooses eat _____

| fruit. |
| meat. |

Their body is covered with ———

| scales. |
| fur. |

They have a long, bushy ———

| nose. |
| tail. |

■ Write a sentence about a mongoose.

_____

_____

Name ______________________________

Resource sheet 9c

■ Complete the wordsearch. You may go across as well as up or down.

m	I	n	n	u	i	t
o	A	r	c	t	i	c
n	A	f	r	i	c	a
g	c	g	n	k	a	r
o	s	l	a	v	e	i
o	e	t	w	h	b	b
s	h	i	g	l	0	o
e	d	e	i	k	c	u

Arctic
mongoose
slave
Africa
caribou
Inuit
igloo

■ Read the words below. Put C beside words that tell you about the Caribbean. Put I beside words that tell you about the Inuit.

Arctic ______ ☐

slave ______ ☐

mongoose ______ ☐

igloo ______ ☐

Greenland ______ ☐

caribou ______ ☐

Africa ______ ☐

Innuit ______ ☐

plantation ______ ☐

Caribbean ______ ☐

Poems with meaningful punctuation

Overall aims

- To revise, identify and name punctuation marks.
- To explore poems with punctuation as part of the meaning.
- To be able to identify similar poems in other anthologies.

Featured book

A Spider Bought a Bicycle and other poems for young children, selected by Michael Rosen, (Kingfisher Books, 1992)

Lesson One

Chosen poem

'The Skyfoogle' (Traditional, adapted by Michael Rosen), (page 72)

Intended learning

- To revise the terms 'capital letter', 'full stop', 'comma' and 'exclamation mark'.
- To explore the chosen poem and how the punctuation helps to express its meaning.
- To be able to identify similar poems in other anthologies.

With the whole class

- Enlarge 'The Skyfoogle'. Read the title to the children and ask them what they think the poem might be about. Read it to them, showing them the text. Try to use intonation and the punctuation to create tension and atmosphere while you read. (At this stage, read it for the 'story content' only.)
- Ask a volunteer to retell the story of the con trick. Make sure that everybody understands what happened in the poem. Ask the children if they can tell you what the Skyfoogle is. (They shouldn't be able to!)
- Together, identify the poem's punctuation. There are exclamation marks, capital letters, full stops and commas. Ask what each punctuation

mark is called. List them on the board. Ask for volunteers to come to the board and draw the punctuation marks beside the list.

- Discuss each verse of the poem. The first verse sets the scene and prepares the reader for the development of the story. The next verse (the longest) builds up the tension and excitement of waiting to see the terrifying creature. The third verse (the shortest) uses mostly monosyllabic words to express the speed and terror of the audience's escape. The final verse deflates the terror, but uses the punctuation to create pauses allowing the reader to realise the trick that has been played.
- Discuss the use of the punctuation in the poem. Some points to be explored are the wide use of exclamation marks, words written in capital letters, the series of full stops and the commas. Ask the children to suggest why capital letters are used for certain words. (For very strong emphasis.) Why are there multiple exclamation marks? (To stir up fear of the Skyfoogle and to create tension.) Why are there commas in the verses? (To help show pauses during reading.) Why are there so many sentences with full stops? (To help show longer pauses and also to build up tension.) Why has the poet used a series of full stops at the end? (For longer pauses, to allow the full impact of the con trick to be realised.)
- Do the children think the punctuation marks help to create atmosphere in the poem? Did they feel tense while they were listening to the poem? Did the punctuation help to make them feel this?

With the lower-achievers

With adult support

Choose from:

1 Read the poem again with the children, encouraging them to join in. Use the punctuation, particularly the capital letters and exclamation marks to create atmosphere. (This may have to be done away from the main classroom!) Ask the children to role-play the events of the poem for a class performance.

2   Look at the list of punctuation marks written on the board during the whole-class session. Ask the children to read them. Challenge them to identify in the poem each type of punctuation mark. Give each child a copy of the poem and ask them to use a different coloured pen to highlight each of the punctuation marks.

3   Using Resource sheet 10a, help the children to insert the words and punctuation in the boxes into the sentences. Give reading support if necessary.

4   Together, look through other anthologies and explore poems that use punctuation for effect. Discuss with the children how the punctuation is used. Keep to one side any poems that you find to share in the plenary session.

5   Make some cards with a punctuation mark on each. Make enough sets for each child to have their own, plus two extra sets. Play a game where you shuffle the cards and deal four to each child. The remaining eight cards should be placed face down on the table. The aim of the game is to make a complete set of the four punctuation marks. The children in turn take a card from the central pile. If they want to keep it they have to discard another from their set. If they don't want it, they replace it at the bottom of the pile. The winner is the first to have a complete set.

Teacher-independent activities

Choose from:

1   Give the children copies of Resource sheet 10a to complete. You may need to read it with them before letting them work on it independently.

2   Ask the children to draw a picture of the Skyfoogle. Remind them that nobody has seen it, so their own imagination can go to work! They should then write a label, a caption or a few words about their Skyfoogle.

3   Ask the children to work in pairs to look through anthologies to find other poems that use punctuation to stress particular points of the poem. Say that they should choose one of them to read at the plenary session.

Plenary session

■   Ask for volunteers to come up and read *The Skyfoogle* with you. (If they can, they could read the poem by themselves!)

■   Let the children who drew a Skyfoogle show their work to the class and explain how they designed their monster. Ask them to read their caption or sentence.

■   Have the children enjoyed exploring this poem? Encourage the children to give reasons for their responses. Did anybody find other poems that use punctuation as part of the meaning? Read out to the class any new poems that have been discovered.

Lesson Two

Chosen poem

'BED!' by Joni Akinrele, (page 73)

Intended learning

■   To explore a different type of poem (a familiar setting) which uses punctuation for effect.

■   To use the poem as a basis for own work.

■   To be able to identify similar poems in other anthologies.

With the whole class

■   Enlarge a copy of 'BED!' Show the title to the children and ask them why they think it is written in capital letters, with an exclamation mark. What do they remember about the use of capital letters and exclamation marks from Lesson One? Remind them about emphasis, atmosphere and effect.

■   Read the poem to the children, letting them see the text. Do any of them recognise this situation? What does their mum, dad or carer do when they nag to stay up? Are there any other familiar situations when they are shouted at for pushing their luck? (For example, closing down the computer, coming in for dinner or getting washed.)

- Look at the poem's punctuation and ask the children to identify what there is. They should name speech marks, capital letters, exclamation marks, question marks and full stops. Invite volunteers to write these on the board. Leave the list up.

- Explore the poem in detail. What are the speech marks used for? Who is speaking in the poem? Why are some words written in capital letters? How do we know that Mum is becoming annoyed? What are the exclamation marks for? Why is there no exclamation mark the first time Mum says 'No', but there is on the next two occasions? What effect does the series of full stops have?

- Do the children think the punctuation helps to put across the meaning and atmosphere of the poem? Encourage the children to give reasons for their responses.

With the lower-achievers

With adult support

Choose from:

1 Allocate roles to the children of the child in 'BED!' and her mother. (This can be done either as individuals or as two groups for unison-reading.) Help the children to read the poem in role. The narrative parts can be read either by you or a third child/group. Practise reciting the poem for a class performance.

2 Using Resource sheet 10b, help the children to write their own poem about being told off at school. They should use punctuation for effect. They can use the words on the sheet to help them. Give reading support where necessary. Remind the children that their poems don't have to rhyme.

3 Using Resource sheet 10c, ask the children to choose their favourite poem of the two featured and then complete the sentences. They may use the words provided to help if they wish.

Teacher-independent activities

Choose from:

1 Let the children complete Resource sheet 10b.

2 Give the children a copy of 'BED!' and ask them to work in pairs. They should use the list of punctuation marks on the board and highlight an example of each in the poem using different coloured pens. They should then label each one with the correct term, for example 'exclamation mark'.

3 Give the children copies of Resource sheet 10c to complete.

Plenary session

- Let the children who completed resource sheets show them to the class and explain what they had to do.

- Ask the children who practised reciting the poem to give a class performance.

- Which of the two poems explored is the children's favourite and why?

THE SKYFOOGLE

There was a man
who turned up round our way once
put up a tent in the park, he did,
put up notices all round the streets
    saying
that he was going to put on show
A TERRIFYING CREATURE !!!!!!
called:
THE SKYFOOGLE !!!!!!
No one had ever seen this thing before.
The show was on for
2 o'clock, the next day.

Next day, we all turned up to see
THE FIERCEST ANIMAL IN THE WORLD
    !!!!!!!!!
The man took the money at the door.
And we poured into the tent.
There was a kind of stage up one end
with a curtain in front of it.
We all sat down and waited.
The man went off behind the curtain.
Suddenly we heard a terrible scream.
There was an awful yelling and crying,
there was the noise of chains rattling
and someone shouting.
Suddenly the man came running onto
    the stage
in front of the curtain.
All his clothes were torn,
and there was blood on his face
and he screamed:
Quick, get out
get out
get out of here.
THE SKYFOOGLE HAS ESCAPED !!!!!!

We got up

and ran out the door
and got away as fast as we could.

By the time we got ourselves together
the man had gone.
We never saw him again.
We never saw our money again either …
… And none of us has ever seen
            THE SKYFOOGLE !!!!!

Traditional, adapted by Michael Rosen

BED!

When it is time to go to bed

my mum says:

'BED!'

I say:

'Please can I stay up

until this film finishes?'

'What time does it finish?' my mum says.

'Ten o'clock,' I say.

'No way,' my mum says.

'Oh can't I stay up for five minutes?'

'NO.'

'Please.'

'NO!'

'Oh ... can't I read in bed?'

'NO!'

'Please.'

'Come here, girl. You are getting on my nerves,

if you are not in that bed

by the time I count to ...'

I walk slowly up the stairs,

my brother is laughing away.

Then my mum starts shouting again.

This time at my brother.

Joni Akinrele

■ Finish the sentences with the words and punctuation that you think are best.

The boy shouted, "Give me the ball, _____"

"No _____" said the girl. "Go away _____"

now	!	!!

··

The dark room felt _____ I was very scared _____.

I ran away _____ _____

!	very fast	spooky

··

An _____ gorilla jumped out at the girl.

"_____ ___", she shouted. The gorilla said, "I just want

to play with you _____".

Help	!	enormous

■ Write a poem about getting told off at school. There are some
words at the bottom of the sheet to help you.

When I got told off

_____

_____

_____

_____

_____

didn't smile	felt bad

didn't do it	wanted to cry

wasn't pleased

said 'Sorry'

it wasn't fair

it was OK

■ Read 'The Skyfoogle' and 'BED!'

■ Which is your favourite poem? Finish the sentences.

_____ is my favourite poem.

I like it because _____

_____

_____

■ Here are some words to help you.

scary	brother	fright
laugh	clever	sister
Mum	like	funny
trick	makes	bedtime

Stories in the first person

Overall aims

- To explore stories told in the first person.
- To distinguish personal pronouns and possessive pronouns.
- To identify short words within longer words.

Featured book

The Baked Bean Cure by Philip Wooderson and Dee Shulman (Collins/Jumbo Jets, 1996)

Story synopsis

Tony is sure that he is going to be burgled and when he hears a crash in the night, it turns out to be the arrival of drippy Uncle Mervyn, a hippy, who agrees to stay and look after Tony and baby brother Ben, while Mum and Dad go away for a break. Tony tries to persuade Uncle Merv to wean Ben off baked beans, and also to ward off the expected burglars. At first everything seems to go wrong: the baby demands even more beans and the house is burgled. But eventually, Uncle Merv's odd habits (obvious to the adult reader!) help to catch the burglars and cure the baby of his bean addiction.

Lesson One

Intended learning

- To become aware of stories told in the first person.
- To use the text as a basis for exploring stories told in the first person.
- To practise changing third person formats to the first person.

With the whole class

- Explain to the children that some stories are written as if the main characters are telling the story to us themselves. How would the narrator refer to himself? Explain that whenever somebody tells a story using the word 'I', this is known as 'the first person'. Write this on the board and leave it up.

- Show the cover of *The Baked Bean Cure* and point to the picture of Tony. Tell the children that this story is written as if Tony is speaking directly to the reader. Ask them how Tony will refer to himself. Read the story with the children, allowing them to see the text, and also the illustrations.

- Explore some of the following ideas: when a story is told in the first person, the storyteller always refer to him or herself as 'I'; the events described by the storyteller have to be witnessed by him or her; the narrator may have knowledge of something that only he or she can have (for example, Tony hears the 'burglars' planning the job, something that Uncle Merv is unaware of); the narrator may be unaware of something that an omniscient author knows (for example, Tony is not initially aware that Uncle Merv's 'Natural Elixir' is Dad's whisky!)

- Briefly look at two or three favourite stories that are written in the third person and show the children how these use 'he', 'she', 'they' and 'it' to tell the story. Ask the children why this is. Explain that these stories are not told directly by one of the characters but by an unseen narrator.

- Write on the board two or three simple sentences in both the first and the third person, for example 'I went to school', 'She jumped off the wall', 'I ate the sweets' and 'He kicks the ball'. Ask for volunteers to come and change these to the first or third person, as appropriate. Try a few verbal examples as well. Point out how the verb often has to change, to agree with the subject. ('He kicks' becomes 'I kick'.)

- Do the children know of any other stories or books which are told in the first person? Encourage them to make a collection of these and leave them on display in the classroom. Let the children explore these at unstructured times of the day.

With the lower-achievers

With adult support

Choose from:

1 Ask the children to choose their favourite episode from *The Baked Bean Cure* and read it together again. Take one or two sentences and

help them to convert them into the third person narrative. Give support with working these out verbally at first and then help them to rewrite them. Draw their attention to any verb changes.

2 Using Resource sheet 11a, help the children to change the sentences that are about Tony, to the first person format. Then ask them to change a sentence or two from the book into the third person format, starting each with 'Tony …'

3 Together, recite familiar nursery rhymes in the first person and ask the children to tell you who is speaking. For example, 'I sat on a wall and had a great fall – all the king's horses and all the king's men couldn't put me together again. Who am I?'

4 Have prepared some simple sentences written in both the first and third person. They should be written on alternate lines. Help the children to rewrite each sentence in the 'other person' format (from first to third person or vice versa).

Teacher-independent activities

Choose from:

1 Ask the children to work in pairs to choose one or two sentences from *The Baked Bean Cure* and then rewrite them in the third person.

2 Give the children copies of Resource sheet 11a to complete.

3 Have prepared some simple sentences written in both the first and third person on alternate lines. Ask the children to work in pairs to change the format to the 'other person'. They should either write the new sentences or record them onto a cassette.

Plenary session

■ Before the plenary session, write a few sentences in both the third and first person on the board. Ask volunteers to come and change them. Did they need to make the verb agree?

■ Ask the children who explored nursery rhymes to explain to the others how they converted the rhymes. Give them the opportunity to recite their new rhymes.

■ Does everybody fully understand the difference between first and third person narrative? If necessary, repeat the main points of the lesson.

Lesson Two

Intended learning

■ To distinguish personal pronouns 'I', 'you', 'he', 'she' and possessive pronouns 'my', 'your', 'his', 'her'.

■ To use the chosen text as a basis for exploring these personal and possessive pronouns.

■ To use other texts for further work on the pronouns.

With the whole class

■ Write on the board 'I', 'you', 'he' and 'she' and ask some of the children to read them. Explain that they are called personal pronouns.

■ Challenge the children to give you examples of some sentences using these pronouns. Start them off with one or two examples such as 'I can jump,' or 'He played football.' Ask the children to give you more examples.

■ Write on the board, under the (appropriate) personal pronouns you have already written, 'my', 'your', 'his' and 'her'. Explain that these are called possessive pronouns.

■ Invite the children to give you examples of sentences using these. Again, you could start them off with one or two examples such as 'My eyes are blue' or 'His dog is very old'. Ask them to write their sentences on the board, using a different colour for the possessive pronouns.

■ Play a game of 'Quick-fire Pronoun Match'. Tell the children they should play as fast as they can. They have to tell you which personal pronoun goes with which possessive pronoun you call out and vice versa. Ask somebody to keep a record of how many correct answers are given in one minute. Challenge the children to beat their own record in the course of several games. Make the game fun and without pressure – be prepared for a lot of noisy shouting out!

With the lower-achievers

With adult support

Choose from:

1   Help the children to write sentences using personal pronouns. They should then write the corresponding possessive pronoun ('my', 'your', 'his', 'her') in a different colour.

2   Using Resource sheet 11b, help the children to complete the sentences with the appropriate pronouns. While the idea is for the personal pronoun and possessive pronoun to agree in each sentence, you could have some fun changing them. For example, 'I wanted to eat her sweets in class.'

3   Together, look through *The Baked Bean Cure* for examples of possessive pronouns. You should find, for example, 'my much-younger brother', 'your cure', 'his jeans' and 'her white T-shirt'. The children should make a list of the examples they find.

4   Look together for possessive pronouns in the pictures on Generic sheets 1 (page 113) and 9 (page 121). For example, 'Who's that sleeping in **my** bed?' and 'There's a lady and **her** dog and a man with **his** child.'

Teacher-independent activities

Choose from:

1   Give the children copies of Resource sheet 11b to complete. You may need to read it with them first before letting them work independently. Explain that the idea is for the personal pronoun and possessive pronoun to agree.

2   Ask the children to work in pairs and look through nursery rhymes for both types of pronouns (for example, Little Jack Horner: he put in his thumb). They can either write their examples or record them onto a cassette.

3   Make some cards with a personal pronoun or a possessive pronoun on each. Make sure that there are at least three copies of each pronoun. The children should play a variation of 'Snap', where the 'snapped' cards are pairs of personal and possessive pronouns. For example, 'I' would be 'snapped' with 'my' and 'she' would be 'snapped' with 'her'.

Plenary session

■   Which are the personal pronouns the class has explored? Ask the children to come and write them on the board. Then invite other children to write the possessive pronouns next to them.

■   If some of the children used a cassette recorder, let them explain to the class what they did and then play the cassette.

■   Play 'Quick-fire Pronoun Match', allowing different children to take the lead.

■   Does everybody understand what personal and possessive pronouns are? Do they understand the difference and what they are used for?

Lesson Three

Intended learning

■   To identify short words within longer words as an aid to spelling.

■   To use the text as a basis for practising this.

■   To use other texts for finding short words within longer ones.

With the whole class

■   Write a long word containing several shorter words on the board – for example, 'standing' contains 'and', 'in', 'an', 'stand' and 'tan'. Write another word on the board, such as 'playground'. Challenge the children to find small words inside this word.

■   Invite the children to suggest some more long words. Write these on the board (or let the children write them). Can they find smaller words in them?

■   Explain to the children that they can learn how to spell more difficult words if they break them down into smaller units. Look at some of the examples on the board and together discuss how they can be broken into 'spelling-sized chunks'.

■   Look through *The Baked Bean Cure* for some more examples: 'watching' contains 'watch', 'at', 'chin' and 'in'.

■ Leave on the board all the words that have been split into smaller parts.

With the lower-achievers

With adult support

Choose from:

1 To give more practice in breaking words into smaller units, continue looking for longer words in *The Baked Bean Cure*. There are examples such as 'straining' ('rain' and 'in') and 'intending' ('in', 'ten' and 'din'). Work closely with the children to find the smaller words within the longer ones. Let them write these on Generic sheet 14 (page 126).

2 Using Resource sheet 11c, help the children to find smaller words in the long words.

3 Make some cards with a word component written on each one. Mix the cards up and spread them out on the table. Help the children to put them together to make the original longer words. You could have cards with the complete words for the children to refer to if necessary.

Teacher-independent activities

Choose from:

1 Ask the children to work in pairs to find long words that can be split into smaller words in other favourite texts. (Make sure the books are at an appropriate reading level.) They should write the long word and the smaller words on Generic sheet 14 (page 126).

2 Give the children copies of Resource sheet 11c to complete.

3 Make some cards with a word component written on each one and let the children play the game described in point 3 above.

Plenary session

■ Did any of the children find new long words which contained smaller words? Ask them to come to the board and write both the long word(s) and the smaller ones. Read all of them together.

■ Ask for volunteers to spell some of the longer words, in small sections. Make sure this is done as a fun activity without any pressure.

■ Was there anything about this lesson that the children found difficult? Encourage the children to respond with reasons.

■ Change these sentences to the first person. They are about Tony in 'The Baked Bean Cure'.

1 Tony found a slug on the dinner.

_____

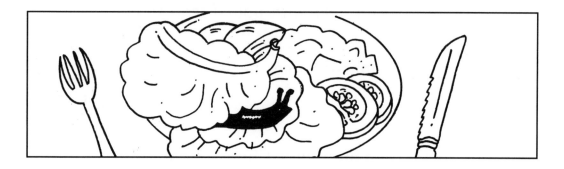

2 Tony had to eat beans for every meal.

_____

3 Tony saw the burglars in the house.

_____

Name _____

■ Write the personal pronouns. Choose from:

I   **You**   **He**   **She**

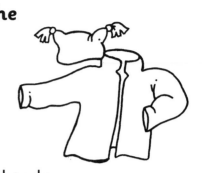

_____ went out with my mum.

_____ put on his coat and hat.

_____ can play with your friend today.

_____ wanted to eat her sweets in class.

■ Write the possessive pronouns. Choose from:

my   **your**   **his**   **her**

You may play with _____ dog.

I want _____ dinner now.

She left _____ computer switched on.

He played with _____ football.

Name ______________________________

■ Find small words in these long words.
Circle them in different colours.

watching	important
together	
morning	playground
supermarket	
something	holiday
window	
information	painting

Stories for characters' behaviour

Overall aims

- To discuss the behaviour of a story's main character.
- To use speech marks appropriately in writing.
- To use dictionaries and word banks appropriately and efficiently.

Featured book

Burping Bertha by Michael Rosen (Andersen Press, 1993)

Story synopsis

Bertha discovers that her mega-burps can send things flying everywhere. She decides to have some fun and uses her belching skills to sort out playground problems, unpleasant teachers and even a boring Christmas concert at school. She hits the headlines and is soon a national celebrity. Hollywood hears of her amazing feats and she is soon an international superstar. Disaster strikes when her plane crashes, however, and Bertha is seen no more. But that is not the end of the story, as rumours abound that Bertha is alive and well and burping happily somewhere… so say her fans!

Lesson One

Intended learning

- To discuss the behaviour of a story's main character.
- To use the featured text as a basis for this.
- To use other favourite texts to explore a character's behaviour.

With the whole class

- Show *Burping Bertha* to the children and ask somebody to read the title. Invite the children to suggest what the title might tell us about Bertha's behaviour. How do we view burping in our culture? Explain that in some cultures, to burp aloud after a meal is considered to be a compliment.

- Read the story to the children letting them see the text and illustrations.

- Ask the children which was their favourite part of the story and why. Make a list of incidents and decide which is the most popular. Why is this? Is it because Bertha does rude things or is it because she uses her 'rudeness' (burping skills) to do humorous things? Are the children glad that various characters in the story get their comeuppance because of Bertha's burping?

- Explore some of Bertha's behaviour and discuss it with the children. Was Bertha's initial burp deliberate? Why did she learn to burp deliberately? What do the children think of this? Why did she use her burp on the boys/the apples/the circus act/Mr Fobnitch? Do the children approve of this behaviour? Encourage them to say why or why not. If they had this skill, how would they use it?

- Ask the children to imagine how the story would be if Bertha did not have the ability to burp. What would have happened in each of the incidents? For example, would Mr Fobnitch change his behaviour? Use these ideas as a way of illustrating how Bertha's behaviour actually contributes to and influences the events in the story. Reread some passages from *Burping Bertha* and ask the children how the other characters in the story react to her behaviour. How are they influenced by it?

With the lower-achievers

With adult support

Choose from:

1   Continue to discuss Bertha's behaviour with the children. Ask them what they think of Bertha's behaviour, for example naughty, funny, rude, clever and fair. Talk about other people's behaviour. Who do they know who is kind, naughty (be careful feelings aren't hurt here), quiet, noisy and so on?

2   Help the children to write their own newspaper headline and draw a 'photograph' of Bertha's exploits, similar to those in the story. Let them refer to the relevant pages of the book if they want to. They could make up a different adventure if they prefer.

3   Using Resource sheet 12a, help the children to identify the different behaviour that is shown in the picture. Read the words with them and ask them to match the words to the children in the picture. Which behaviour do they like best?

4   Together, read other texts and explore the behaviour of the main characters. Help the children to make a list of descriptive words. Discuss together how the behaviour of the character(s) influences the story. Ask them to suggest how the story would be different if the character's behaviour was different.

Teacher-independent activities

Choose from:

1   Give the children copies of Resource sheet 12a. Ask them to work with dictionaries to find the words on the sheet. They should then match the words to the children in the picture.

2   Ask the children to work in pairs to choose a favourite fairytale. They should decide how the story would be different if the character's behaviour was changed – for example, if the wolf had been kind and not wanted to eat the Three Little Pigs what would have happened? Let the children either write a sentence or record their conclusion onto a cassette.

3   Give the children the following words written on cards or the board: bad, good, kind, silly, naughty and brave. They should work in pairs to discuss and agree under which of these headings various fairytale characters belong, according to their behaviour in the stories.

Plenary session

■   Why is a character's behaviour so important in a story? Make sure that all the children understand that the whole course of a story is influenced by this. Invite the children to say what influence a character's behaviour might have on another character.

■   Ask the children who completed the resource sheet to tell the class about the different types of behaviour they found in the picture.

■   If any of the children made cassette recordings, encourage them to share them with the class.

■   If any children explored other texts ask them to tell everybody what they found out about the characters' behaviour.

Lesson Two

Intended learning

■   To use the text as a basis for revision of work on speech marks.

■   To look at other texts for other ways of presenting speech.

■   To use speech marks appropriately in writing.

With the whole class

■   Remind the children of the work done in Year 2 on speech marks. Ask if they remember how speech marks are written. Invite volunteers to draw these on the board: " – ", ' – ' and speech bubbles.

■   Choose two or three spoken sentences from *Burping Bertha*. Write one of them on the board with no punctuation. Read it with the children pointing to each word as you do so. Now ask for a volunteer to come up and put in the punctuation. Does everyone agree? Did that child use single or double speech marks? Say that it could have been done using either.

■   Do the same with another spoken sentence from the book and a different volunteer to write in the speech marks.

■   Ask the children where they can find other speech marks – comics, plays, newspaper quotes, magazines, poetry and so on.

With the lower-achievers

With adult support

Choose from:

1   Look through *Burping Bertha* with the children, encouraging each of them to find an example of speech. Read these aloud together, helping the

children to read in role while you read the narration. Help the children to write their example in the speech bubbles on Generic sheet 2 (page 114), or on Generic sheet 3 (page 115), remembering to use speech marks. They can check against the original for accuracy.

2   Help the children to complete Resource sheet 12b. Together, choose the type of speech marks (" – " or ' – ') they should use. Give reading support if necessary.

3   Ask the children to tell you phrases that they use on a regular basis – for example, 'Cool', 'No way', 'It's a goal!' and 'I don't want to!' Help them to write these with speech marks using Generic sheet 3 (page 115).

Teacher-independent activities

Choose from:

1   In pairs, let the children complete Resource sheet 12b. You may need to read it with them before letting them work independently.

2   Ask the children to work in pairs to look in a comic for a few examples of speech. They should write the speech from the comic's speech bubbles in linear form and include the speech marks. They could use Generic sheet 3 (page 115) for this.

3   Provide slips of paper with spoken sentences from *Burping Bertha* written on them. Ask the children to write in the speech marks. They can check these afterwards against the text.

Plenary session

■   Ask for volunteers to come to the board and write an example of punctuated speech.

■   Ask the children who found examples of speech in comics or magazines to show these to the class. Encourage them to point out the speech marks and tell you which ones they are (speech bubbles or inverted commas).

■   Does everybody understand how and why we use speech marks? Was there anything difficult about the lesson? What activities did the children enjoy most and why?

Lesson Three

Intended learning

■   To revise alphabetical order.

■   To use dictionaries appropriately and efficiently.

■   To use the featured text to practise dictionary skills.

With the whole class

Make sure an alphabet frieze is displayed while working on this lesson.

■   Tell the children that they are going to do some work on alphabetical order. Write several letters at random on the board. Ask for volunteers to put these into alphabetical order. Encourage the children to come to the board and order the letters correctly themselves.

■   Ask the children where they will see words in alphabetical order. Make a list. Suggestions might include dictionaries, encyclopedias, telephone directories, maps and indexes. Leave the list on the board.

■   Look at a dictionary with the children. Show them the alphabetical order of initial letters and then explain that second and subsequent letters of a word are then ordered alphabetically. Write on the board a few words with different initial letters and a few with the same initial but different second letters, for example 'man', 'dog', 'tap', 'leg', 'lip' and 'look'. Invite volunteers to write the words in order on the board.

■   What other uses does a dictionary have? For example, giving a definition, helping to spell, giving synonyms and explaining the origin of a word. List these on the board and leave the list there but cover it before the plenary session.

■   Ask some of the children to choose two or three words from *Burping Bertha* and together look for these in the dictionary. Read the definitions with the children.

With the lower-achievers

With adult support

Choose from:

1   Make sure the children understand the concept of alphabetical order. Repeat the activity of putting single letters into alphabetical order. Start with three or four letters and gradually increase the number. Let the children refer to the alphabet frieze if necessary.

2   Give the children copies of Resource sheet 12c to complete. Give support if necessary.

3   Using alphabet cards, give each child a card. Ask them to stand next to each other in alphabetical order of their cards. Do this several times by changing their letters. Ask if they would stand in the same order if they went by the initial letters of their first names. Encourage them to explain why.

4   Choose two or three words from *Burping Bertha* with different initial letters, and two or three with the same initial letters but different second letters. Ask the children to put these into alphabetical order. Can they do this with the title of the book? Work closely with them to look for the words in the dictionary. Help them to write the definitions.

Teacher-independent activities

Choose from:

1   Give the children copies of Resource sheet 12c to complete. You may need to read the instructions with them before letting them work independently.

2   Ask the children to work in pairs. They should choose one sentence from *Burping Bertha* and order the words alphabetically by initial letter or initial and second letters. Warn them that the result will not make sense!

3   Ask the children to make a collection of classroom items and display them in alphabetical order. They should write labels for the objects. Ask them to look for the words in the dictionary and write the definitions.

Plenary session

■   Gather the children together for the plenary session by asking them to join you in alphabetical order (by initial letters of their first names).

■   Ask the children who reordered sentences from *Burping Bertha* alphabetically to read these aloud.

■   Did the children find it difficult to order words with the same initial letter but different second letters? What other books did they use or find during their activities that are ordered alphabetically?

■   Ask for the different uses of a dictionary. Uncover the list written in the whole-class session. Did the children leave anything out?

■ Look at this picture. How are the children behaving?

■ Match these words to the children in the picture.

rude   helpful

kind   careless   naughty

nice   angry

■ Fill in the speech marks for these sentences.

There was once an egg-man.

He said, Hello. My name is Humpty Dumpty.

He climbed up on a wall and said, I like it

up here!

Suddenly he slipped.

Help!   he shouted.   I'm falling off!

He fell and broke into pieces.

Now I'm an omelette,   he said.

A B C D E F G H I J K L M N O P Q R S T U V W X Y Z

■ Put these letters into alphabetical order.

F   M   D   S   Z   A   C   W

_____

■ Put these objects into alphabetical order.

man   hat   pen   dog   tin

_____   _____   _____   _____   _____

■ Put these words into alphabetical order.

slip   show   stop   smell

_____   _____   _____   _____

■ Look for these words in a dictionary and write what they mean.

man _____

pen _____

tin _____

Stories for characters' feelings

Overall aims
- To analyse the feelings and emotions of a story's characters.
- To explore words that indicate a sequence or passage of time.
- To revise the long vowels from Key Stage 1.

Featured book
The Magic Finger by Roald Dahl (Puffin Books, 1974)

Story synopsis
The little girl (who is not named) has a special power in her finger that metes out punishment on anyone who makes her angry. The story tells how the Gregg family, who are very fond of hunting and shooting, are forced by this power to change places with the wild duck they have spent the day trying to kill. They quickly learn the horrors of being hunted and spend a terrifying night waiting for the worst to happen. They manage to eventually return to normal, only after vowing faithfully never to hunt wild creatures again. The little girl who has the magic finger is happy to see her friends restored to normality, but then feels 'the urge' coming on when she discovers that other neighbours are out enjoying a day's shooting...

Lesson One

Intended learning
- To understand the concept of feelings or emotions.
- To analyse the feelings and emotions of the story's characters.
- To use other texts to discuss the feelings of the characters.

With the whole class
- Write 'feelings' on the board and read it with the children. What does 'feelings' mean? Ask them to think of another word that means the same ('emotions'). Look in a dictionary for 'feelings' and 'emotions' and discuss with the children what the dictionary says.
- Ask them to give you examples of types of feelings. Write these on the board. They may suggest 'sadness', 'anger', 'joy', 'embarrassment' and so on. Leave the list on the board.
- Tell the children that they are going to explore a story where feelings play an important part. Read *The Magic Finger*, letting them see the text and illustrations.
- Ask the children what emotions were felt by the little girl at the beginning of the story, for example anger at the Greggs and sympathy for the animals. How did the Greggs feel at the beginning? They enjoyed hunting, they felt contempt for the little girl and they had a disregard for the animals. Ask the children to comment on how these feelings had changed by the end of the story. Make a list on the board of all the feelings suggested by the children that are in *The Magic Finger*.
- Look at some of the illustrations. Discuss the facial expressions and how these show us the emotions being felt by the person in the drawing. How can we interpret somebody's feelings by their face?
- Explore some fairytales and the characters' feelings. For example, how would Snow White have felt when her stepmother was being unkind? How would the stepmother have felt when the mirror told her she was the most beautiful? How would the Seven Dwarfs have felt when they found Snow White apparently dead?

With the lower-achievers
With adult support
Choose from:

1 Discuss again the emotions that are explored in *The Magic Finger*. For example, the little girl is amazed at the power in her finger, she is angry at the Greggs and she is sympathetic towards the animals; the Greggs are unconcerned about wildlife, mock the little girl and feel terrified when they are turned into birds. Let the children refer to the list written during the whole-class session to give them a start.

2   Using Resource sheet 13a, help the children to match the emotions to the pictures. Give reading support if necessary. Encourage them to write a sentence for one or two of the words. They could use Generic sheet 3 (page 115) to write out the sentences, for example 'She was sad because she had lost her cat.'

3   Prepare a set of cards with an emotion word written on each. Play a game where the children have to read their card and make a facial expression to show the emotion word. If somebody guesses the emotion correctly, they win a counter or tiddlywink. The winner is the child with the most counters at the end of the game.

4   Together, explore some more fairytales. Discuss the emotions felt by the characters as various things happen to them. Make a list and see how many emotions are common to several stories.

Teacher-independent activities

Choose from:

1   Divide a sheet of paper into four and write 'sad', 'happy', 'scared' and 'sorry' in the sections. Ask the children to draw a face in each section and write a sentence for one (or more) picture(s).

2   Give the children copies of Resource sheet 13a to complete.

3   Ask the children to work in pairs to choose two or three fairytales. They should decide what feelings the characters would have. For example, how did Cinderella feel at different stages of the story? They could draw pictures of the different stages of the story and label them with the emotion words.

Plenary session

■   Ask the children who explored fairytales to share with the class what they found about the emotions of the characters.

■   Has anybody found new emotion words? Invite them to come to the board and add them to the list.

■   Do the children understand the important part that the characters' emotions play in a story?

Lesson Two

Intended learning

■   To explore words that indicate a sequence or passage of time.

■   To use the featured text to illustrate the use of such words.

With the whole class

■   Ask the children to retell the story of *The Magic Finger* in their own words. Make a note of any words they use such as 'next', 'then', 'after that' and so on. When they have finished telling the story, write on the board any words that the children used which indicated the passage of time.

■   Ask them what happened in their retelling when they used these words. Explain that they moved the story on to the next phase. Encourage them to tell you some more words or phrases that do this, such as 'the following day' or 'the next time'. Invite some children to write these on the board.

■   Tell the children that Roald Dahl (and indeed all authors) used words and phrases like this to show how time passes. In *The Magic Finger*, he used 'the next morning', 'in the next hour', 'a minute later' and 'at last'. Can the children see how these phrases move the story on to the next stage?

■   Look at another well-known story together. Ask the children to identify the words or phrases which show the passage of time. Let them add these to the list. Leave the list on the board while working on this lesson.

With the lower-achievers

With adult support

Choose from:

1   Look at *The Magic Finger* together with the children for other words and phrases that mark the passage of time. Help them to write these and then challenge them to think of some more of their own.

2   Write on the board two or three simple words/phrases. For example 'first', 'then' and 'in the end'. Ask the children to retell the story of a fairytale using these, for example 'First, Cinderella couldn't go to the ball, then she could, then she met the prince and in the end they married.' Help them to write their stories.

3   Using Resource sheet 13b, help the children to read the sentences and put them in order to show the passage of time. They should write the letters next to the correct numbers. Then they have to put the pictures in order by circling the correct number.

Teacher-independent activities

Choose from:

1   Give the children copies of Resource sheet 13b to complete. You may need to read this with them before letting them work independently.

2   Give the children copies of Generic sheet 1 (page 113). Say that they must indicate the order of the story by writing the words 'One day', 'First', 'Then' and 'At last' above the pictures.

3   The children could retell a favourite story by drawing pictures and then writing words below each picture to show how the story moves on.

Plenary session

■   Ask if any of the children found new words or phrases. Invite them to write them on the board (or you scribe if necessary).

■   Ask somebody to explain what would happen if such phrases weren't used in a story. Do the children think stories would be boring if they stood still in time? Encourage them to give reasons for their answers.

■   Ask for a spokesperson from each group to explain what they did. Let the children who completed the resource sheets show them to the class.

Lesson Three

Intended learning

■   To revise the long vowels from Key Stage 1: 'ee', 'ai', 'ie', 'oa' and 'oo'.

■   To consolidate the correct use of the term 'phoneme'.

With the whole class

■   Ask the children if they remember the correct name for the sounds in a word. (Phoneme) Does anybody remember how to spell it? Write 'phoneme' on the board. Before moving on to the next part of the lesson, make sure everybody knows what the term means.

■   Write on the board the vowel phoneme 'ee' and ask the children what it says. Invite them to give you some examples of words containing 'ee'. Encourage them to come to the board and write them. Some examples are 'knee', 'sheep', 'three' or 'squeeze'.

■   Do the same for each of the other phonemes, 'ai', 'ie', 'oa' and 'oo'. Leave the phonemes and the examples on the board while working on this lesson.

With the lower-achievers

With adult support

Choose from:

1   Focusing on one phoneme at a time, ask the children to identify objects in the classroom containing that phoneme. Using Generic sheet 15 (page 127) help them to write in each petal the name of one of the objects.

2   Using Resource sheet 13c, ask the children to supply the missing phoneme from each word. Help them to write a sentence for each word/picture.

3   Make some cards with one of the phonemes written on each card. (Each phoneme should be in duplicate or triplicate according to the size of the group.) Let the children play a game with a 'Draughts' board and counters. They

take a card, read the phoneme and read one of the words written on the board for that phoneme. If they are correct, they move their counter forward on the 'Draughts' board. The winner is the first to reach the opposite side of the board.

Teacher-independent activities

Choose from:

1   In pairs, let the children complete Resource sheet 13c. They should use dictionaries to help them write the sentences.

2   Ask the children to work in pairs. They should record onto a cassette as many words as they can that contain each of the phonemes. Challenge them to write some of the words as well.

3   Ask the children to make mini books, one for each phoneme. Each child could take one phoneme. They should find words with their phoneme in them and write them in the book and illustrate them.

Plenary session

■   Let the children who recorded words onto a cassette play it to the class. Invite the children to add new words to the list by coming to the board and writing them down.

■   Say each phoneme one at a time. Ask for volunteers to come to the board and write the phoneme. Ask other children to name the phoneme again as it is being written.

■   Make sure everybody understands what 'phoneme' means. Ask a child for its meaning.

■ Look at the pictures and read the speech bubbles.

■ Match the words to the pictures.

scared

angry

happy

worried

sad

■ Read the sentences and write their letters in the correct sequence.

A   Next I made a sandcastle.

B   One day I went to the beach.

C   At last I went home.

D   I swam in the sea first.

1 _____   2 _____   3 _____   4 _____

■ Show the correct order of these pictures to tell the story by drawing a circle around the correct number.

1 2 3 4

1 2 3 4

1 2 3 4

1 2 3 4

■ Write the missing phoneme in each word.

ee   ai   ie   oa   oo

b __ t   tr __ n   b __ ts

fl __ s   sh __ p

■ Write a sentence for each word.

_____

_____

_____

_____

_____

Poems for humour

Overall aims

- To compare different types of humour in poems.

- To express preferences and justify these.

- To use humorous poetry as a basis for own work.

Featured books

There's an Awful Lot of Weirdos in our Neighbourhood by Colin McNaughton (Walker Books, 1990)

A Third Poetry Book compiled by John Foster (Oxford University Press, 1982)

Lesson One

Chosen poems

'Teef! Teef!' and 'I Don't Want to go into School' by Colin McNaughton, (page 101)

'I went to the pictures tomorrow' (Anon), (page 101)

Intended learning

- To explore poems that tell a story or portray a situation in an amusing way.

- To express preferences and justify these.

With the whole class

- Enlarge copies of 'Teef! Teef!', 'I Don't Want to go into School' and 'I went to the pictures tomorrow'.

- Tell the children that they are going to explore some poems that are intended to make them laugh, although they may not find all of the poems funny since humour is very personal. Explain that what one person finds very funny may not be at all amusing to somebody else.

- Read 'Teef! Teef!' with the children, letting them follow the text. Did they find it funny? Why? Some of the following ideas could be discussed: the poem is written as though a toothless person is speaking, so some sounds are substituted such as 'f' for 'th' and 'sh' for 's'; the

title and first line are a pun on 'thief', since the poem is dealing with the theft of the person's dentures; the line 'shomebody shtole them from/Under my nose!' is a play on words, since the theft of dentures would be literally that.

- Read 'I Don't Want to go into School' with the children. Did they find it funny? Why? Did they expect the speaker in the poem to be the headmaster? Who did they think it was while you were reading the poem? Some of the following ideas could be discussed: the humour comes in the surprise at the end; the verses are written as a dialogue between Mum and her son; the son uses language like a child whining for his own way – this makes the surprise at the end even funnier.

- Now read 'I went to the pictures tomorrow' with the children. Did they find this one funny? Why? The following ideas could be discussed. This is a nonsense poem. Why? All the lines contradict themselves.

- Ask the children which poem of the three was their favourite. Discuss the reasons for their preferences.

With the lower-achievers

With adult support

Choose from:

1 Read the poems together again, encouraging the children to join in when they can. Discuss the poems with them – do they make them laugh? Why or why not? Do they like an element of surprise to make them laugh? Do they like nonsense poems? Do they like funny poems that are about people? Ask them which of the three is their favourite and why. Help them to write a silly poem of their own, perhaps based on 'I went to the pictures tomorrow'.

2 Using Resource sheet 14a, help the children to read the sentences and tick the boxes when they agree. Help them to write their sentences.

3 Decide on one of the poems to learn – let the children choose which one. Then allocate a line (according to ability) to each child (or several children in groups to recite in unison).

4   Share some other humorous poems and discuss why they are amusing. Is there anything consistent about the poems that most of the children find funny? For example, do they think poems about teachers are the funniest? Or poems with a surprise element?

Teacher-independent activities

Choose from:

1   Record the poem 'I Don't Want to go into School' on cassette before the lesson. Let the children work in pairs and allocate the roles of the headmaster and his mum. They should role-play the poem while listening to the recording.

2   Let the children complete Resource sheet 14a. They could work in pairs to do this.

3   Ask the children to work in pairs and look through an anthology of humorous poetry. They should choose one or two favourites to record on cassette tape.

Plenary session

■   Ask the children who learned to recite one of the poems or those who recorded poems onto tape to give a performance.

■   Read the other two poems again, encouraging the children to join in. Do they still find them amusing? Has anybody discovered more poems that are humorous? Ask them to share these with the rest of the class.

■   Ask the children who role-played 'I Don't Want to go into School' to show the other children their acts.

Lesson Two

Chosen poems

'Rockabye baby' by Max Fatchen, (page 102)

'Little Jack Horner' and 'A Poem for Bella' by Collette Drifte, (page 102)

Intended learning

■   To explore poems that are amusing versions of traditional rhymes.

■   To express preferences and justify these.

■   To use humorous poetry as a basis for own work.

With the whole class

■   Enlarge copies of 'Rockabye baby', 'Little Jack Horner' and 'A Poem for Bella'.

■   Tell the children that today they are going to explore some more humorous poetry, but different from that in Lesson One.

■   Read 'Rockabye baby' with the children letting them follow the text. Did they find it funny? Why? Discuss some of the following ideas: there are substitutions for words in the original rhyme such as 'treetop'/'stairtop', 'rock'/'stop'; 'The way that she's pinned' refers to the baby's nappy; 'It's simply the wind' is a pun on the wind of the original rhyme and the baby's trapped wind of this version. Which of the two versions do the children prefer? Why?

■   Read 'A Poem for Bella' with the children. Did they find it funny? Why? Discuss some of the following ideas: this poem is called a limerick (don't discuss the actual structure in detail but explain that many limericks start with 'There was a …' and follow this format); the humour in this poem comes from the fact that Bella has married a monkey; it is also funny because we know this, but she doesn't.

■   Read 'Little Jack Horner' with the children. Did they find it funny? Why? Discuss some of the following ideas: this is another example of a well-known nursery rhyme being changed; the humour lies in the different food that Jack is eating and his reaction to it; there is a surprise element because the reader thinks he knows what's coming next but, of course, the rhyme is different. Which of the two versions do the children prefer and why?

■ Tell the children that you are all going to write a class version of another nursery rhyme. Decide together which rhyme to rewrite (or you could use the version of Humpty Dumpty on Resource sheet 14b to start you off). Remind them that the new poem doesn't have to rhyme, but it does have to be humorous. Brainstorm ideas together and write on the board key words that can be used. Decide together how the final version of the poem and write it on the board. Leave it up while working on this lesson.

With the lower-achievers

With adult support

Choose from:

1 Read each poem together again, encouraging the children to join in. Remind them that 'Rockabye baby' and 'Little Jack Horner' are rewritten versions of nursery rhymes and 'A Poem for Bella' is a limerick. Which of the three do the children find the funniest and why? Ask them if there are any they do not find funny and encourage them to give reasons. Help them to write a sentence about this.

2 Using Resource sheet 14b, read the new version of 'Humpty Dumpty' together, giving reading support if necessary. Remind the children of the class version of a rewritten nursery rhyme. Help them to write their own version of 'Humpty Dumpty'. Remind them that it does not have to rhyme. They could use the words at the bottom of the sheet to help them.

3 Look through other anthologies for limericks. Discuss these with the children. Then help them to write their own limerick on Resource sheet 14c. They can use the words on the sheet or their own. (Don't insist on a rhyming limerick at this stage.)

Teacher-independent activities

Choose from:

1 Let the children complete Resource sheet 14b and/or 14c.

2 Ask the children to work in pairs to practise reciting the rewritten version of one of the nursery rhymes ('Rockabye baby', 'Little Jack Horner' or 'Humpty Dumpty'). They should choose which one they want to learn. Let them use the enlarged copies.

3 Let the children record the rhymes. They could either take a line each or a rhyme each.

Plenary session

■ Let the children who practised the new versions of a nursery rhyme give a recital for the other children.

■ Let some of the children who worked on the resource sheets share their new versions with the others.

■ Has anybody found another humorous poem during group activities? Encourage them to tell the rest of the class about it or read it to the others.

Teef! Teef!

Teef! Teef!
I've loshed my teef!
Hash anyone sheen my teef?
You won't be able to help, I shuppose;
But shomebody shtole them from
Under my nose!
Hash anyone sheen my teef?

Colin McNaughton

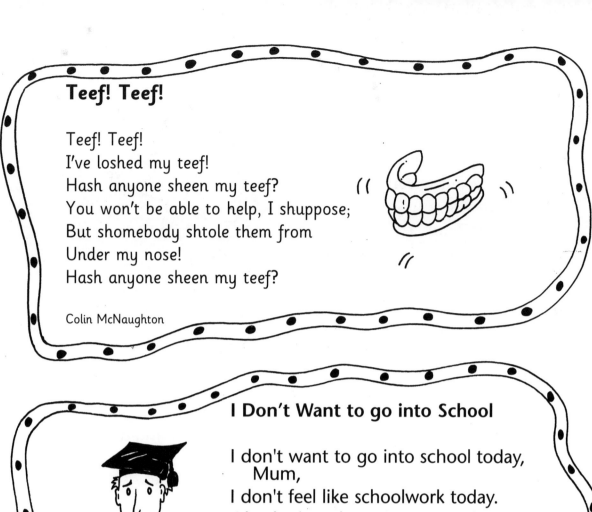

I Don't Want to go into School

I don't want to go into school today,
   Mum,
I don't feel like schoolwork today.
Oh, don't make me go into school today,
   Mum,
Oh, please let me stay home and play.

But you must go into school, my cherub,
   my lamb.
If you don't it will be a disaster.
How would they manage without you,
   my sweet,
After all, you are the headmaster!

Colin McNaughton

I went to the pictures tomorrow

I went to the pictures tomorrow
And took a front seat at the back,
A lady she gave me an apple,
I ate it and gave it her back.

Anon

Rockabye baby

Rockabye baby
On the stairtop,
Crying and screaming
When will it stop?
Is it her temper?
The way that she's pinned?
Rockabye baby
It's simply the wind.

Max Fatchen

Humpty Dumpty

Humpty Dumpty sat on a wall,
Humpty Dumpty had a great fall.
All the king's horses and all the king's
   men
Had scrambled eggs for breakfast again.

Anon

Little Jack Horner

Little Jack Horner sat in a corner
Eating some worm-and-snail pies,
He put in his thumb and then pulled
   out some
Slugs, and said, 'I prefer flies!'

Collette Drifte

A poem for Bella

There was a young lady called
   Bella
Who wanted to marry a fella,
But the guy that she wed
Was a monkey instead
Of a man and no one dared tell
   'er.

Collette Drifte

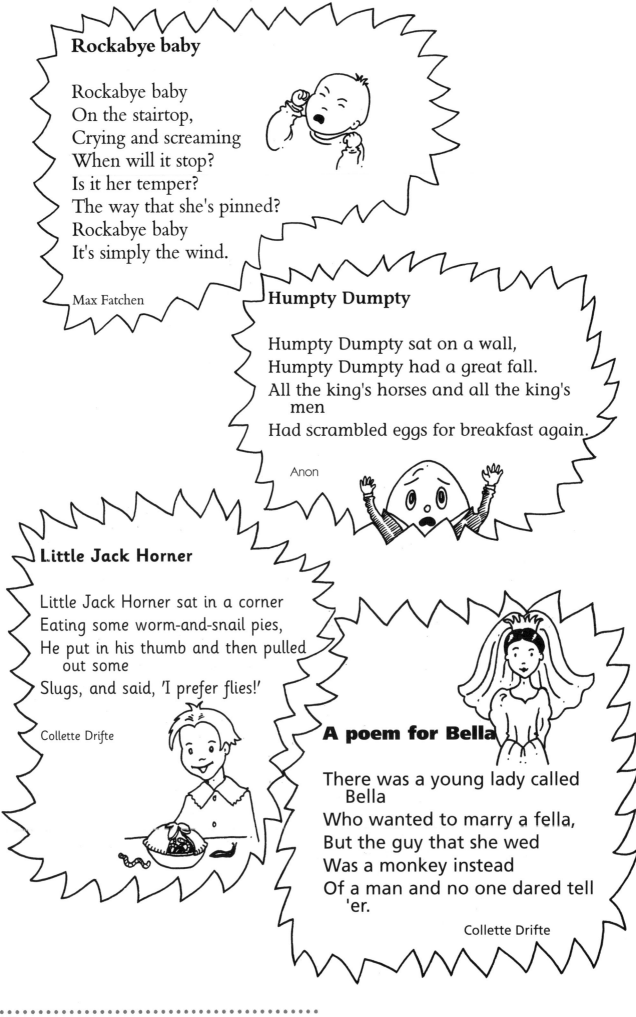

■ Read 'I Don't Want to go into School' by Colin McNaughton.

Tick ✔ the boxes that you agree with.

I was surprised at the end of the poem. ☐

I don't like poems about school. ☐

I knew what the end would be. ☐

A funny poem about teachers is good. ☐

■ Now finish this sentence. Cross out the words you don't need. The words in the box might help you.

I thought the poem was/was not funny because _____

_____

_____

_____

_____

| didn't | usual | expect | behave | want |
| wonder | silly | adult | pretend | child |

■ Read this poem.

> Humpty Dumpty sat on a wall,
>
> Humpty Dumpty had a great fall.
>
> All the king's horses
>
> And all the king's men
>
> Had scrambled egg
>
> For breakfast again.

■ Write your own Humpty Dumpty poem. You can use the word bank below or choose your own.

Humpty Dumpty sat on a _____

Humpty Dumpty had a _____.

All the _____

And all the _____

Had _____

For _____

chair	big	dinner	egg and chips
teachers	children	big scare	lunch

■ Choose from the words below to write your own funny poem. Add some of your own words too.

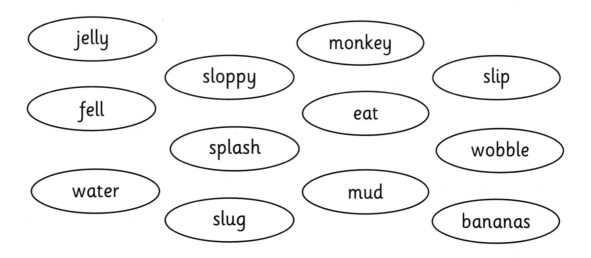

There once was a _____

That _____ in the _____

The _____

And _____

_____

■ Decorate your poem with a border.

Poems to create effect

Overall aims

- To understand and use the term 'onomatopoeia'.

- To explore the chosen poem that creates effect through the use of onomatopoeia.

- To use the poetry as a basis for own work.

Lesson One

Chosen poem

'The Sound Collector' by Roger McGough © 1990, (page 109)

Intended learning

- To understand and use the term 'onomatopoeia'.

- To explore the chosen poem that creates effect through the use of onomatopoeia.

With the whole class

- Enlarge a copy of 'The Sound Collector'.

- Tell the children that you are all going to read a poem about sounds and that the poem contains lots of sound words. Ask them what they think you mean by 'sound words'. Encourage them to give you examples of what they think you mean. Write some of these on the board if they are approaching the concept of onomatopoeia.

- Read 'The Sound Collector' with the children, letting them follow the text. Ask them what they think the poem is about. Do they think the poem is real or fantasy? Why? Ask them what the poet means at the end of the poem when he says, 'Life will never be the same.'

- Write 'onomatopoeia' on the board. Read it to the children. Explain that this is the word we use to describe the use of words that sound like their meaning. For example, 'Vrrroooooom' for a car engine or 'plop' for a drop of water falling into water. Invite the children to give you some more examples. Write these on the board and leave them up.

- Tell the children that 'The Sound Collector' is full of onomatopoeia. Explain that the onomatopoeic words used in the poem echo the sounds of everyday living that we are often totally unaware of. Agree together some of the onomatopoeic words from the poem. Ask for volunteers to come out and write them on the board or point to them on the enlarged copy of the poem.

- Challenge the children to make up some onomatopoeic words of their own. Make a list of these or ask them to write their own examples on the board.

With the lower-achievers

With adult support

Choose from:

1   Read 'The Sound Collector' again with the children. Ask them to tell you some of the onomatopoeic words used in the poem. Help them to make a list of these. Invite them to say which their favourite words are and why. Help them to choose one favourite and write a different sentence using that word.

2   Remind the children that in 'The Sound Collector', the stranger took away the sounds of that morning. Work together to decide some sounds that could be included in the poem if the stranger had come later in the day. For example, if he had come at lunch-time, include sounds such as the children playing at lunch break or the whistling of the window cleaner and so on. Help them to write the sounds they suggest.

3   Using Resource sheet 15a, ask the children to match the onomatopoeic words to the pictures. Give reading support if necessary. Ask them to write more new words. They could be completely new words they have made up. Help them with any onomatopoeic spelling.

4   Allocate one line from the poem to each child. Decide together beforehand which verse(s) they would like to learn. Help them to learn their lines and put them together to recite the verse(s). Encourage them to speak the onomatopoeic words with expression in a way that puts across the sounds.

Teacher-independent activities

Choose from:

1 Let the children complete Resource sheet 15a. You may need to read the words with them before letting them work independently.

2 Ask the children to work in pairs to make a word wall containing all the onomatopoeic words from 'The Sound Collector'. They should write one word in each brick of the wall, for example 'turning', 'ticking' and 'crunching', each in a separate brick.

3 Ask the children to work in pairs to make up some onomatopoeic words connected with the classroom, for example the scraping of chairs on the floor, the squeaking of the pen/chalk on the board or the swishing of the venetian blinds.

4 Ask the children to choose two or three favourite lines from the poem and write these in their poetry books. They could then illustrate these. Alternatively they could record them making the onomatopoeic words sound effective.

Plenary session

■ Ask the children whether they can remember the word for 'sound words'. Make sure all the children can say 'onomatopoeia' and know what it means.

■ Ask the children who made up their own onomatopoeic words to tell the class about them and how and why they chose the sounds of the words. Invite them to write their words on the board.

■ Ask the children who learned some verses from 'The Sound Collector' to recite them for the class. Then ask them to recite them again, encouraging the rest of the class to join in where they can.

Lesson Two

Chosen poem

'The Sound Collector' by Roger McGough © 1990, (page 109)

Intended learning

■ To reinforce the term 'onomatopoeia'.

■ To use the poetry as a basis for own work.

With the whole class

■ Remind the children of 'The Sound Collector' and ask them to remember what it is about.

■ Ask them to remember the term for words that express a sound. Remind them of 'onomatopoeia'. Invite them to give you some further examples. Ask for volunteers to write these on the board.

■ Tell the children that they are going to look at 'The Sound Collector' once again and think about how it might help them to write their own onomatopoeic poems.

■ Divide the class into groups and read 'The Sound Collector' in a round, each group reading one verse in turn. (If possible, practise this for a school assembly performance.)

■ Write four or five onomatopoeic words from the poem on the board. Ask the children to suggest alternative sources for these noises. For example, 'hissing' could be a snake ('frying-pan' in the poem), 'bubbling' could be soup cooking ('bathtub' in the poem) and 'squeaking' could be a mouse ('chair' in the poem). Write these alternatives on the board.

■ Together, decide on a subject for the class poem. Some ideas might be 'Bonfire Night', 'The Swimming Pool' or 'The Zoo'. Brainstorm onomatopoeic words, list them and then together decide the form of the poem. Write it on the board and leave it up while working on this lesson. You could model writing an ABC poem, for example 'A is for an angry ant, B is for babbling baboons, C is for crunching crocodile teeth.'

With the lower-achievers

With adult support

Choose from:

1 Look at the class poem again and work with the children to make up another verse. They should make a list of the onomatopoeic words the group chooses or makes up, and include them in the new verse. Give support where necessary.

2 Using Resource sheet 15b, help the children to write their own sound poems about 'Bonfire Night'. They could use the words in the boxes or choose their own. Remind them that their poems don't have to rhyme but that there should be onomatopoeic words in them.

3 Using Resource sheet 15c, help the children to write their own onomatopoeic word under each picture. Encourage them to think of some other words to write on the back of the sheet. They could illustrate these.

Teacher-independent activities

Choose from:

1 Let the children complete Resource sheet 15b. They should have access to dictionaries and a thesaurus for this activity.

2 Ask the children to work in pairs and, using Resource sheet 15c, make up some onomatopoeic words for each picture. They should try to write the words. Alternatively, they could record their words on a cassette. (Writing and spelling their onomatopoeic words could be difficult without adult support.)

3 Divide a sheet of paper into four sections and at the top of each section write one of the onomatopoeic words from 'The Sound Collector'. Ask the children to work in pairs to write in each section as many things as they can which could also be associated with that word. For example, 'crunching' could be snow, toast, biscuits, gravel and so on.

Plenary session

■ Let the children who made up poems and who would like to share them with the others, read or recite them to the class.

■ Ask the children who made up onomatopoeic words to read them to the class and write their words on the board or play their cassette. Alternatively, make a phonics game by encouraging the class to spell the new words as they sound.

■ Make sure everybody fully understands the meaning of 'onomatopoeia' and can use the term correctly.

The Sound Collector

A stranger called this morning
Dressed all in black and grey
Put every sound into a bag
And carried them away

The whistling of the kettle
The turning of the lock
The purring of the kitten
The ticking of the clock

The popping of the toaster
The crunching of the flakes
When you spread the
    marmalade
The scraping noise it makes

The hissing of the frying-pan
The ticking of the grill
The bubbling of the bathtub
As it starts to fill

The drumming of the raindrops
On the window-pane
When you do the washing-up
The gurgle of the drain

The crying of the baby
The squeaking of the chair
The swishing of the curtain
The creaking of the stair

A stranger called this morning
He didn't leave his name
Left us only silence
Life will never be the same.

Roger McGough

Name _____

■ Join the onomatopoeic words to the pictures.

popping

hissing

crunching

purring

mooing

swishing

ticking

drumming

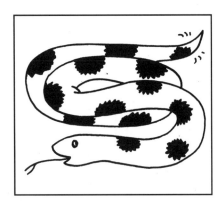

■ Write some
of your own.

_____

_____

_____

_____

_____

■ Write your own sound poem. You can the use the words in the boxes or choose your own. You don't have to use all the lines.

<u>Bonfire Night</u>

_____

_____

_____

_____

_____

tinkle	thud	hiss	hum
crack	rumble	bang	crash
whistle	wheeee	whoosh	zoom

■ Look at the pictures and write an onomatopoeic word under each one.

_____   _____

_____   _____

_____   _____

■ Write words with the correct number of syllables in each box.

1 syllable	2 syllables	3 syllables

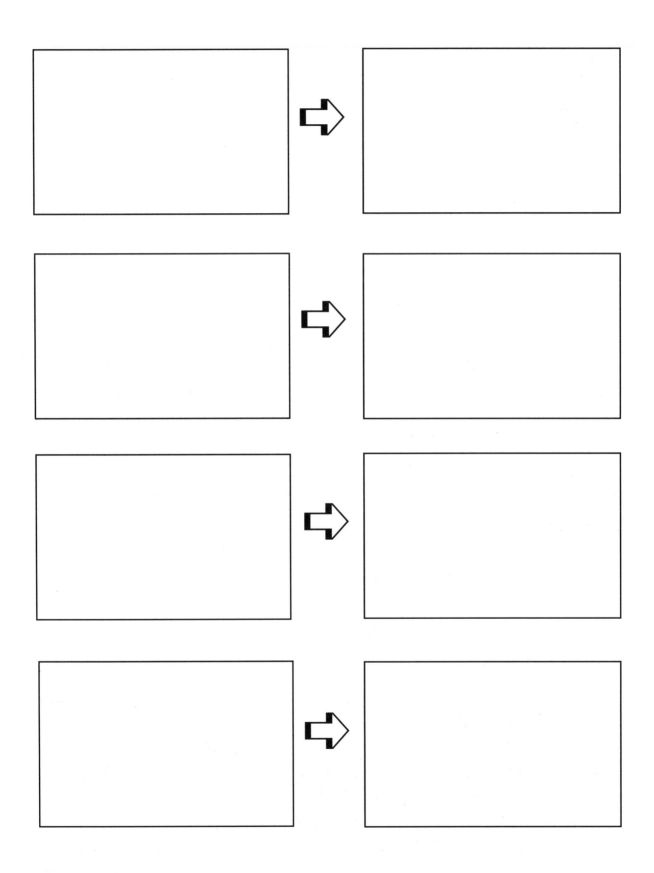

One day ...

It was very quiet ...

Last Monday ...

Once upon a time ...

In the winter ...

Yesterday morning ...

It was a very hot day when ...

Tomorrow ...

■ Read the adjectives. Write some verbs and some nouns
to go with them.

_____ old _____

_____ red _____

_____ fast _____

_____ high _____

_____ big _____

_____ sweet _____

_____ fat _____

■ Cut out the circles.

■ Pin circle 2 to circle 1 with a split pin.

■ How many contracted words can you make?

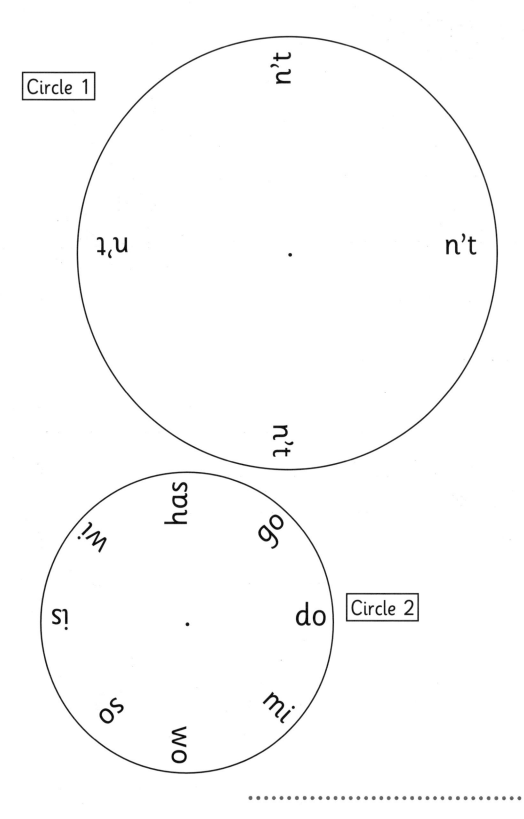

■ Follow the numbers.

1 Learn the words at the bottom of the page.

5 Write

_____

_____

_____

_____

_____

6 Check

fold back

- -

2 Look

_____

_____

_____

_____

4 Cover

3 Say

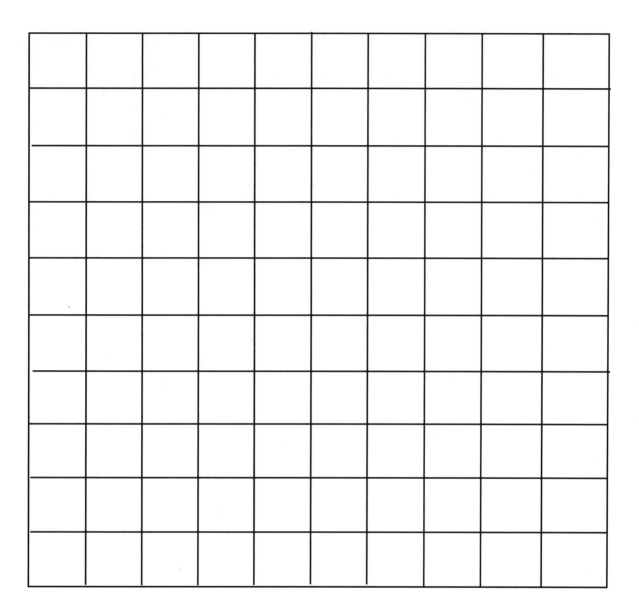

■ Smaller wordsearches or crosswords can be made by blanking
off columns and rows before photocopying.

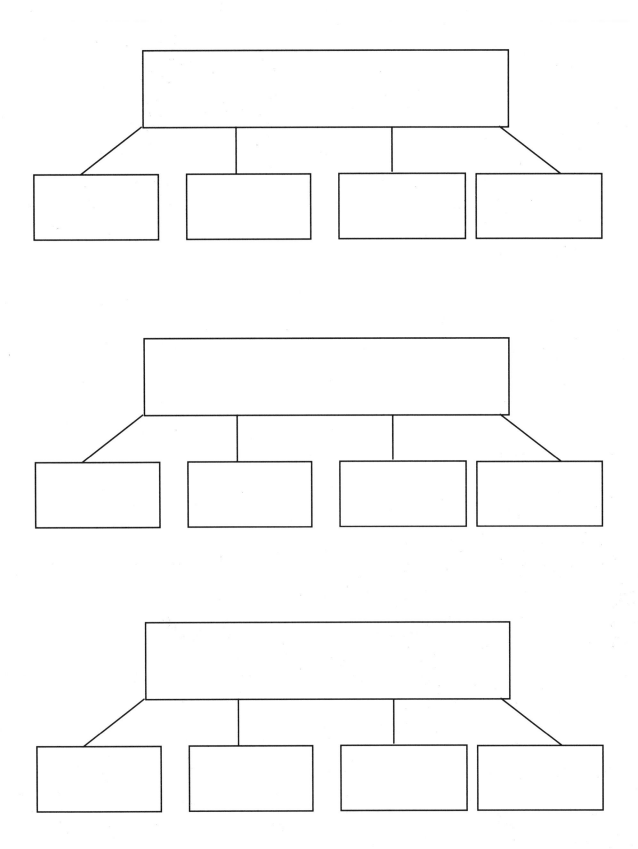